AF701968

# Democracy and Social Justice

# Democracy and Social Justice

## *Uncollected Writings of Louis Brandeis*

By

**Louis D. Brandeis**

Edited by

**Peter Scott Campbell**

CAROLINA ACADEMIC PRESS

Durham, North Carolina

Library of Congress Cataloging-in-Publication Data

Names: Brandeis, Louis D., 1856-1941, author. | Campbell, Peter Scott, editor.
Title: Democracy and social justice / edited by Peter Scott Campbell.
Description: Durham, North Carolina : Carolina Academic Press, 2025. | Includes bibliographical references and index.
Identifiers: LCCN 2025000983 | ISBN 9781531032647 (paperback) | ISBN 9781531032654 (ebook)
Subjects: LCSH: Equality before the law--United States. | Discrimination--Law and legislation--United States. | Race discrimination--Law and legislation--United States. | Social justice--United States. | Strikes and lockouts--Law and legislation--United States. | Price fixing--Law and legislation--United States. | Brandeis, Louis D., 1856-1941--Political and social views. | Democracy--United States.
Classification: LCC KF4755 .B73 2025 | DDC 342.7308/5--dc23/eng/20250114
LC record available at https://lccn.loc.gov/2025000983

Carolina Academic Press
700 Kent Street
Durham, North Carolina 27701
(919) 489-7486
www.cap-press.com

Printed in the United States of America

# Contents

# Introduction

Few Supreme Court justices have had a greater impact on modern life than Louis D. Brandeis. His court opinions, of course, have shaped the law and have helped articulate many rights Americans enjoy today. But Brandeis was a prolific author before he ascended onto the Court and much of what he wrote then continues to be relevant today. The threat of monopolies, the importance of unions, and the obligations of citizens living in a democracy are just a few of Brandeis's interests that still affect Americans.

Many of Brandeis's pre-Court writings have been collected in *Other People's Money*, *Business—A Profession*, *The Curse of Bigness* and *Brandeis on Zionism*, all of which are still read today. But even those four books did not collect all of Brandeis's work. In the decades since those books were published more of Brandeis's writings have been uncovered. Some have been found in old newspapers that escaped the notice of scholars and biographers, while other unpublished works have been discovered in archives.

*Democracy and Social Justice* collects many of those works in an effort to expand Brandeis's corpus as well as to re-introduce him to a new generation of readers. The title of this book reflects two themes of much of the work collected here and in much of Brandeis's work as a whole. As the son of immigrants who fled Europe for the freedoms offered in America, Brandeis was a lifelong proponent of democracy and its promise of equal rights to all. Any person, or institution, that threatened a person's right to freedom and self-improvement was not just an affront to that person, but also to democracy itself.

And in Brandeis's view, one of the biggest threats to democracy was trusts—business combinations so large that they stifled free enterprise and kept their workers locked in a form of peonage. Their control of the markets was so complete that they could keep prices artificially high, drive competitors out of business, and could stifle any union's attempt to improve their workers' lives. Brandeis's insights into these inimical practices were so influential that they helped usher in new anti-trust legislation that guided American economic policy for decades. A governmental backlash against breaking up monopolies set in a while ago and undid much of that work, but a new generation of economists have rediscovered Brandeis's writing and are working to bring back his vision. Hopefully, this book will guide them and future economists in that work.

Much of the writing in this book deals with Brandeis's fight against trusts. He spent much of his time during the lead up to the 1912 presidential election campaigning against them. A number of those speeches are collected here, one of which is being published for the first time. He also spent many years fighting against a railroad company's attempt to control all the transportation in New England. Two of his speeches from the fight are here, including one that has never been published before.

Labor unions are another example of Brandeis's love of democracy. The ability of workers to band together to fight for improved working conditions was, for Brandeis, a perfect example of democracy in action. The articles collected here touch on the threat posed to unions by trusts and how strong unions could help improve businesses.

The rest of the articles touch on miscellany of topics, such as price-fixing, suffrage, racial discrimination, the proper role of lawyers in society, and a history of the Harvard Law School. Of special note is a memoir Brandeis dictated to his secretary that laid untouched in the archives at Brandeis University. There is also a transcription of a conversation held late in Brandeis's life that was found among Brandeis's papers held in the Louis D. Brandeis School of Law at the University of Louisville.

Many people assisted me with the compilation of this book. Kurt Metzmeier and Erin Gow provided invaluable service as proofreaders and advisors. Sarah Shoemaker and Chloe Gerson from the Robert D. Farber University Archives and Special Collections were excellent guides to the collection of Brandeis papers at Brandeis University. And Laura Rothstein and Les Abramson from the University of Louisville, and Mel

Urofsky, Brandeis researcher par excellence, have been fantastic mentors during all my years of studying Brandeis. This book would not have been possible without any of them.

# Democracy and Social Justice

# 1

# Practicing Law

*Brandeis gave this speech to the Harvard Law Society on March 28, 1915. Despite its title, this is not a piece of advice for improving one's practice of law. Instead, it is a condemnation of the rise of the corporate attorney and a paean to the joys of independent practice. This speech has never been published. The original manuscript is stored in folder WB22663 in the Louis D. Brandeis papers at the University of Louisville. Footnotes have been added to cite to the references made in the speech.*

You are entering upon the practice of the law at a time of peculiar promise. After a long period of decline, our profession is rising again in dignity and public estimation. This is true both of the practicing lawyer and of the courts.

For the bar there was the grand period which de Tocqueville described in 1825.[1] Then with the development of our industries and financiers came the unfortunate change which Bryce described in 1889.[2] And Bryce noted a further depression twenty years later.[3]

---

1. Brandeis says 1825, but the first English edition of *Democracy in America* was published in 1835. Alexis de Tocqueville, *Democracy in America* (London: Saunders and Otley, 1835), pp. 135–147.

2. James Bryce, *The American Commonwealth*, 2nd ed. rev. (London: Macmillan and Co., 1889), pp. 719–721.

3. James Bryce, *The American Commonwealth*, New Ed. (New York: The Macmillan Co., 1910), pp. 916–918.

Our courts suffered a similar decline in public estimation during the first half of the nineteenth century. The judges of the state courts were quite commonly men of character, learning, and ability. The change from an appointive to an elective judiciary was attended by a marked deterioration in the quality of our judges. The method of selection and the resulting uncertainties of tenure lessened the attractiveness of the bench to able men, and on the other hand, private practice was becoming relatively lucrative through our great industrial development. The position of judge was regarded rather as a steppingstone to success in practice than the culminating reward for success at the bar.

The bench reached perhaps its lowest plain in public estimation a few years ago when the demand for the recall of judges and of judicial decisions became insistent.

The decline in the bar began sometime after the introduction of the custom under which great corporations and financiers had their lawyers instead of great lawyers their clients. The development of the corporation attorney was natural, but it was not beneficent. The great interests needed the best legal advice and needed it frequently. They could afford to pay the cost, however high, of acquiring it; and lawyers, ever appreciative of good retainers, supplied the demand.

Lawyers were attracted not only by the lure of gold, but by the power incident to representing a great corporation, and the distinction then also incident to close association with money kings and captains of industry. For a long time, neither businessmen nor lawyers appreciated that the new relationship would impair both the standing and the usefulness of the lawyer.

Judgment is the most valuable of the qualities supplied by lawyers; and to sound judgment there are, among others, these essentials: detachment and breadth of experience.

The position of the exclusive corporation lawyer, whether it be that of the obviously dependent house attorney, or that of the eminent and nominally independent counsel, is both blinding and narrowing. We see things in just proportion only from a reasonable distance. The general counsel, particularly when he is also a director, often disqualifies himself from exercising sound judgment by participating in the very matters upon which he should give independent advice. It was a wise saying that "The man who is his own lawyer has a fool for a client;" and to some extent a director-lawyer is his own client. Besides, the lawyer's judgment was often impaired also by the excessive specialization involved in becoming a general counsel of a large corporation.

Enlightened businessmen are beginning to recognize that in many relations in life they can be better served by a lawyer with less detailed knowledge of their particular business, who has a wider experience, and who is free from possible prejudices. In other words, by men who lead instead of following instructions. And enlightened lawyers are beginning to find the narrow field of activity unsatisfying and often irksome. This feeling is intensified by the fact that to an ever greater extent the problems of business have come to involve questions of public policy, and the corporation counsel find themselves at times obliged to advocate professionally courses of action with which, though they are not improper, are not personally in accord. There are marked evidences of revolt on the part of lawyers of high standing and ability against occupying positions however remunerative, which involve such consequences, and such revolt is more common among younger men.

The number of businessmen and lawyers who take this newer view are still relatively few, but the evidence of change of attitude on this subject is unmistakable. No doubt corporations and financiers will continue to have their attorneys, but they will be attorneys who hold positions more similar to those occupied by the solicitors in England, and the lawyers of ability, of wide vision and with higher professional aims and ambitions will be free as the English barristers have remained throughout the development of power in spite of the industrial advance.

The recent progress with our courts is perhaps even more marked than that at the bar. The most obvious defects in our courts were lack of administrative efficiency, and lack of appreciation of their social function. A great advance in administrative efficiency was made when, about ten years ago, courts began more generally to recognize that decisions should be reversed and new trials granted only where errors made appeared to have resulted in wrongs to the litigant. The great advance of the courts in social efficiency is of more recent date. But the decision rendered last month by the New York Court of Appeals in the One Day Rest in Seven case[4] shows how even that hitherto ultra-conservative court has come to appreciate the force of social and economic facts.

4. *New York v. C. Klinck Packing Co.*, 108 N.E. 278 (1915).

With the multiplication of the professions, including the profession of business, the lawyers has had to meet considerable competition. But the attractions which it offered to those selecting an occupation—the opportunities for wealth, for fame, and for usefulness in public and private affairs, are as great as ever. Indeed, the industrial revolution is making demands upon our lawyers for services which are no less important and are far more pervasive than those rendered a century ago when the Federal Constitution was first being interpreted. Social and political science have opened to the lawyer a field of activity as thrilling as that occupied during the past generation by the physician, the chemist and the engineer; and his field is even broader, for the lawyer has occasion in adjusting human relations to apply all that those scientists developed.

2

# Protect Law-Abiding Business

*During the early days of the 20th century, public dissatisfaction over the creation of trusts and the inability of the Sherman Act to dismantle them began to grow. Several bills that sought to amend the Sherman Act were introduced by Robert La Follette and other Progressive senators. During 1912 and 1913, Brandeis gave a series of speeches in support of these acts and against the existence of trusts. On January 3, 1912, Brandeis gave this speech to a group of businessmen in Chicago. It was reprinted in the January 27 and February 3 issues of* La Follette's Weekly.

Mr. Chairman and Gentlemen: Those who have got on the committee that is working with Senator La Follette are apt to think of him first as a man of affairs, a man of large affairs, and then as a constructive statesman. They think of him as a man peculiarly safe to follow because the measures which he advocates are based upon facts, and he possesses in a peculiar degree the capacity to know and appreciate facts.

He has a diligence in the pursuit of knowledge and a retentiveness of memory which make it easy relatively for him to know what existing conditions actually are, and what past conditions, out of which present conditions have grown, have been. And he has a vision which enables him far-sightedly to see the trend of the inevitable result of these facts.

He is not a man who has legislated on general principles deduced from some general ideas and conceptions. He is a man who looks at existing and past conditions with a view of determining how they shall be remedied, and what the measures are by which this can most effectively be done.

As illustrating this point of view of Senator La Follette's, I want to speak to you of his proposed treatment of the great social and industrial questions involved in the trust issue.

Senator La Follette, recognizing, as everyone in the country recognizes, the unsatisfactoriness of the present situation, undertook to find out why it was the trust question is disturbing business and is leaving unsatisfied the demands of the people throughout the country.

He took up, therefore, in an animated way, this effort to find out what it was which made people here, there, and everywhere, complain of the present situation with respect to the Sherman Anti-Trust Law.

Now what did he find?

He found that the first and almost universal complaint, in view of the recent decisions of the Supreme Court declaring that only restraints in trade that were unreasonable were illegal, was of *uncertainty in the application of the law*. Men did not know what they could do and what they could not do, and in that uncertainty, business was disturbed generally, and the particular plans of individuals were subject to great disconcertion.

Now, having found that uncertainty is one of the causes of discontent, he proceeded in an eminently practical way to remove, so far as was possible, the elements of uncertainty.

By looking over, by studying the field of experience with trusts as developed in everyday business during the last twenty one years, since the Sherman Act came into operation, to determine what it was that we were able, in light of that experience, to clearly declare to be unreasonable, and to find out what could be so laid down as unreasonable, he undertook to set up those acts as the red lines of danger for the man in business, which he should be taught to avoid.

He found as a result of that study and experience what is perfectly obvious: *that what is unreasonable are those acts which have for their end not a continuance, but a destruction of competition; those acts of unfair conditions which in one way or another are designed not to develop business, but to destroy competitors.*

The conduct of the Standard Oil Company affords us multitudinous examples of cutting prices in one locality to destroy a competitor there, while prices are left high in another locality.

The Tobacco trust, by going into certain districts and giving away goods, destroys a competitor.

Or, again, take the acts of these trusts which we call espionage and bribery of employees to disclose trade secrets in order that the trusts might get an unfair advantage.

The La Follette anti-trust bill, which is a supplement rather than an amendment of the Sherman law, undertook in various ways to remedy these evils and give certainty to the interpretation of the law, so that the complaint that men did not know what was permitted and what was not permitted under that law could be removed.

Then the next point to which Senator La Follette addressed his attention in the construction of that bill was the complaint so commonly made that prosecutions under the law were often futile on account of the length of time involved in the case because of the way in which it was conducted, and the production of evidence regarding whether restriction of trade was a reasonable or unreasonable act.

And so, turning to a very simple and recent analogy, we find that under the Interstate Commerce act the great problem which was constantly before the shipper when increases in rates were attempted was the necessity for proving that the proposed increase was unreasonable.

The law of 1910, in securing the enactment of which Senators La Follette and Cummins took so large a part, made this change among others: *That when a railroad undertook to increase rates, the burden of proof to show the reasonableness of the increase should be upon the railroad company instead of the shipper, because the railroad company would possess all the evidence and could with ease produce most of the facts bearing upon that subject.*

It was by virtue of that provision that we were enabled, early in 1911, to secure from the Interstate Commerce Commission that decision upon the advanced rate case which denies the general increase that was proposed. The railroads failed to convince the Commission that their proposed increase was reasonable.

In the same way the La Follette bill proposes that when there is a restraint of trade as a result of combination, that those who assert that that restraint of trade is reasonable have the burden of presenting the evidence and proving the facts.

That simple provision will make almost a revolution in the speed with which these inquiries relating to the Sherman law can be disposed of, because every company must stand ready at any time to prove that its acts, since they do restrain trade, are reasonable, that is, are beneficial to the public and make for the general welfare.

The third respect in which Senator La Follette undertook to improve the defect in the existing situation as to the Sherman law is this: Everyone who has considered the operation of that act has pointed to what rises almost to a condition of scandal in the futility of a law of Congress which has been upon the statute book for twenty-one years.

The most that anyone can claim for a Supreme Court decision in cases such as the Standard Oil and Tobacco Trust is that it may prevail upon the corporation from restraining trade illegally.

*But what becomes of all the past twenty-one years of violating of the law which resulted, on the one hand, in amassing for the stockholders of those companies hundreds of millions of dollars and, on the other hand, has resulted in crushing by illegal means hundreds and perhaps thousands of competitors?*

Nothing is of such significance to us at the present time as respect for law, and yet there is no phenomenon in all the land that is so provocative of disrespect of the law as is this situation. The Supreme Court of the land, by unanimous decision, has condemned these great corporations, which they declare to be illegal by reason of the ruthless acts of destruction of competitors; yet all of these competitors are without redress. They have gone on suffering year after year; they have been crushed out of existence, *yet those who have been found guilty of the act go free.*

After the Tobacco Trust decision, the common stock of the Tobacco company in a time said to be a time of general depression in business, a time in which business and railroad stocks were at a much lower figure than they have been in previous years—the stock of the Tobacco company rose to a point the highest in its record!

Now, if you read that situation, appreciating the injury, the dangers, to the community of such a blemish upon our legal system, you will appreciate that the La Follette bill undertook in a perfectly simple, practical way the betterment of the situation.

Why is it that today those who suffered from the Tobacco Trust's illegal operations have no remedy?

I will tell you. The Sherman law gives ample remedy on paper. It provided that anyone who had been damaged from the illegal actions of the trust *could recover triple damages.* That was merely a paper provision, because he who was being crushed or had been crushed could not stand up and conduct the litigation against these great trusts. Human resources were absolutely inadequate in such a case. Therefore, one after another, absolutely helpless, lay down practically to die, buried beneath the heavy rule and burden. If any there were who now would undertake to raise themselves and say, in the light of these decisions, "We want redress," the statute of limitation steps in and stops them.

There is nobody in this country, no individual man, who can compete with these huge corporations. The government through its Bureau of Corporations making the investigations—the government, on behalf of the people, can bring that corporation, that great trust, to its proper position. But when the government has established the facts by these investigations and prosecutions, then it has determined the facts not only for the purpose of state, but also for the purposes of everybody who has been injured. And when that decision is rendered then everybody who has been injured may go into the court and say, "I was injured, my business suffered three, four, five hundred thousand dollars loss; give me my remedy!"

*The moment such a proceeding is begun by the government, the statute of limitations ceases to run against any American citizen.*

Whether the litigation is conducted for five or ten years, as some have been, nevertheless at the end of that time, when the Supreme Court renders its final decision, the day of accounting comes, and the great trusts must account to the American people for all the damage they have done.

This is simply the practical business way that La Follette has of dealing with a business proposition. There are many more provisions in that bill designed in just that way to facilitate the law enforcement and to secure for the American people what they undertake to secure.

Now, I want to speak for a little while, if I may, upon the other question which Senator La Follette had to consider when he took up the trust question. It is the underlying question whether the people of the United States want that which the Sherman anti-trust bill was confessedly enacted for the purpose of carrying out.

The Sherman law proceeds upon this fundamental proposition: *It is to the interest of the people of this country that competition shall prevail and that private monopoly shall not control business.*

That was the proposition enacted almost by universal consent as the American principle, twenty-one years ago.

Now, when the Supreme Court decisions in the Standard Oil and Tobacco trust cases made that law of vital effect, when it held up to the American business man that the principle which had been declared in the law of Congress was going to be enforced, every statesman undertaking to deal with the situation had to make up his mind definitely whether that principle of the Sherman law was sound or whether it was unsound; whether the idea that competition was the life of trade, that competition made liberty and welfare, was a proposition that was true, or whether it was one of those scattering generalities, true principles at one time which however had become obsolete in the great industrial world.

Senator La Follette undertook to deal with the inquiry in the same practical way in which he dealt with the details of the law which Congress had enacted. He directed his inquiry along these lines:

*What about the strong assertion of men high in business that there are advantages in monopoly?*

*Are there advantages in monopoly which counter-balance the disadvantages?*

*Are the wastes of competition inevitable wastes, or are they merely the ordinary incidents of life subject to regulation?*

These are questions not properly the subject of philosophic speculation but of investigation, questions which are to be solved by looking into facts and talking about facts rather than talking about principles.

There are certain principles which La Follette recognized, and as a statesman and man of affairs he had to look at.

They were these: That there were two kinds of efficiency, which we must exact from the great business institutions and indeed from all affairs of the country.

One is economic efficiency. The other is social efficiency.

In order to determine the proper basis for this trust question, La Follette said: "We must look into both these questions and see what the answer is. Are these trusts really economically more efficient than the independent businesses? Or are they not? And what also is the social efficiency of the trusts?"

Now, his investigation into the economic efficiency of the trusts disclosed what I believe to be a clearly defined proposition, that instead of being economically efficient as they are declared to be, they are distinctly inefficient; that the supposed efficiency of these trusts, when examined in the light of their experience during the last ten years, will be shown to be a delusion.

There are trusts which have been immensely remunerative, which have accumulated hundreds of millions of dollars surplus and have distributed hundreds of millions among stockholders, but these are trusts which have obtained that result not through economic efficiency, not through being able to produce or distribute at a lower cost than their competitors, *but those that were able to obtain that end through the control of prices, as the Standard Oil controlled prices.*

It is a fact that these great trusts make a profit four to eight times that which is an ordinary rate of profit in the independent business. These great prosperous corporations demonstrated their greatest efficiency in making people pay prices which under no other circumstances they would have had to pay. When you turn from this trade-dominating trust to the trusts that have merely obtained high prices but have never risen to the point of controlling the situation you have an entirely different result. You have there a situation where competitors have a market steadily encroaching upon the trusts; taking from the trusts much of their business.

Take the Sugar trust. At the time of the much-discussed Knight decision,[1] twenty years ago, the Sugar trust held 95% of the American market; last year the report of the Sugar trust disclosed that it held a trifle over 42 per cent of the American market, and comparing that situation with the previous year you would see that constant ebb of business from the Sugar trust to their competitors.

Turn from the Sugar trust to the greatest of all trusts, the Steel trust, and you have exactly the same predominance. With all the power that the Steel trust wields, not only through its control of the steel and iron and ores, but also through its great financial adjuncts, this trust has gone exactly the same way in respect as the Sugar trust.

As everyone knows, the Steel trust since its organization has been adding to its plants and increasing its facilities for production by taking over other companies, and yet the United States Steel Corporation in 1911 has a much smaller proportion of the steel business of the United States than it had in 1901. Its competitors, many of them relatively small competitors, have, by virtue of those advantages which inhere in individual ownership and smaller plants, made tremendous strides upon the domains of the Steel trust, though they had to pay fearful tribute in the

1. *United States v. E. C. Knight Co.*, 156 U.S. 1 (1895).

shape of higher rates, and were subject to a rise in the price of ore which is almost a revolution in this country.

Not only that. When you examine the statement of the United States Steel Corporation compared with its previous years, you will find that there is a marked decline in the rate of the earnings of the Steel trust upon its invested capital, as compared with the earlier years of its life; and when you turn to another basis of investigation, its foreign trade, upon which the Steel Corporation prides itself, when we come to direct competition with what other industrial countries, notably England and Germany, have been doing during the past ten years, you have a most marked demonstration of the lack of efficiency on the part of this steel corporation, with all of its great resources.

Probably every one of you can remember the situation regarding the foreign steel trade as it presented itself eleven years ago. Germany and England were almost in a panic at the invasion of their markets and the distribution of the business of those markets of our invasion. They said, "This industrial invasion will destroy our business."

Then came these great combinations. When you look at the situation ten years later you see this: You see that we in the United States—notably the Steel Corporation which dominates the situation—that the Steel Corporation has so increased its own cost of producing iron and steel that our contribution to the great markets of the world outside of Germany and England has been almost negligent, while at the same time Germany has increased its export trade almost five times, and England has increased its exports also to a very large extent.

Germany exported 1,800,000 tons in 1900 and in 1910 it exported nearly 5,000,000 tons. We had at the time of the formation of the Steel trust 1,154,000 of exports and last year we had 1,534,000 and during those years in which Germany, and also England—despised England!—were increasing their export business, there laid idle on the average of the Steel Corporation's capacity nearly one-third of its plant.

The only reason we did not take more business in 1909 was that we lacked furnace capacity to do it. In 1910 we had enough spare furnace capacity in the United States to supply the whole of the export demands of Europe outside of Germany and England. That business, which is anybody's business who can take it, is 10,000,000 tons. We had 10,000,000 tons unused capacity in 1910!

And why was it? It was because as an incident to these huge corporations, as an incident to this terrible over-capitalization, as an incident to this extraordinary increase (what the English term this "ridiculous" increase) in the price of ore in America, we were unable to compete, and Germany and England, in spite of this world wide increase in cost, have been able to produce their iron and steel at no greater cost than they did in 1889.

Now this inability of the Steel corporation to keep down costs manifests itself to men in its inability to meet the demands of the public in trade and transportation, in a better article than was being supplied.

The railroads with their heavier engines and cars and denser traffic and faster trains, demanded steel rails that would meet the tests and demands of time.

How has that been? In the railroad world you will find during the last four years constantly growing complaint of the defective rails. The complaint has grown to such a point as to make necessary an investigation by the Interstate Commerce Commission. Doubtless many of you have seen the figures on this subject. They show that during the ten years since the organization of the Steel corporation, instead of getting an increase in efficiency and production, we have a situation of derailment increasing from 72 accidents in 1902 to 249 in the year 1910. That is the record on the part of that trust and will be found to be true in many respects in regard to other trusts on the economic situation.

We pass from the economic side to the side which is even more important—the social side. Of social efficiency you find a result that is even more damnable than that described. You find that these two profits extracted from the American people have been used not to improve the condition of the hundreds of thousands of American citizens who are gathered together in the organization as workers to make the wealth of our people, but are used to crush them and fasten upon these employees the power of the huge corporations.

I want you to think of these problems and to think of the way La Follette thinks of them, by looking into the exact facts. Not only to see what is and what is not the record of business but to act upon that record in reaching the conclusion which we have in view.

That method is the safe method. It is the method Mr. La Follette has pursued in all his legislation which has made Wisconsin the envy of so many.

What he has done in his state and what he has done in Congress he would do in every position of trust in which he may be placed, and no position, in my opinion, can be too high for a man who understands as he does the needs of the American people, who feels as he does brotherhood with them, and the great brotherhood of them in a way that I believe no American has done since Abraham Lincoln.

3

# Labor and the New Party Trust Program

*In this speech, Brandeis speaks out against the lax attitude Theodore Roosevelt's party had about trusts and the dangers this posed to unions. (At the time of this speech, Roosevelt's party was known as the New Party. It would become known as the Bull Moose Party later.) The speech was given to the Massachusetts branch of the American Federation of Labor and was published in the October 12, 1912 issue of* La Follette's Weekly.

The coming presidential election is of supreme importance to the workingman. It is he who suffers most from existing abuses. It is he who has most to gain from a change for the better. It is he who has most to lose from a change for the worse. Fortunately, you working men have not only the right to be heard on the pending issues, but you have, by reason of numbers, the power, in large measure, to determine those issues if you utilize the power which you have.

The possession of that great power imposes upon you and your fellow workingmen a grave responsibility—the duty of considering carefully for yourselves, your wives, your children, and for the whole community, what each political party has to offer, and to cast your ballots, only after examining carefully, and weighing dispassionately what each of the parties may, under existing leadership, be expected to perform.

The questions raised by the several platforms and by the character and acts of the several candidates are numerous and many of these questions are important. But there is one issue which is fundamental and which, particularly for the workingman, overshadows all others in importance. That issue is this: industrial liberty, or industrial despotism.

I propose to devote the time which you have so kindly allotted to me, to the discussion of this single issue; to discuss the subject only so far as it affects the labor problem; and, as the real contest is now between the Democratic Party and the New Party, I shall further limit my discussion to the difference between these two parties on this issue. The Democratic Party stands for [the] liberty and justice the New Party attempts to secure.

The New Party presents a platform in many respects admirable. It is broad and comprehensive; it is clear and direct in its declarations of principle; it is definite in its statement of the measures which it advocates. It sets forth some principles with which every intelligent, well-meaning American must heartily agree. It proposes many measures which would mark real progress. The New Party's advocacy of these principles and measures must cheer the heart of every workingman, as it does mine. The platform is admirable, also, in this: it declares in effect that the principles enunciated and the measures proposed are not merely planks in a platform to be discarded as old lumber after the election is over. It declares they are solemn covenants; that they are the terms and provisions of a contract by which the party and its leaders are to be irrevocably bound, and which they pledge themselves to enforce if elected to office. All this is as it should be.

But for the very reason that this platform is broad and comprehensive, that it is clear, direct and definite in its provisions, and that it is offered to you as a contract to be accepted or rejected by you—examine it carefully. Study particularly its effect upon labor. And in making that examination note not only what it contains, but what it omits; and consider what the natural results will be of the policies which it advocates. And when you make that examination, you will find that there is a significant omission; and that this skillfully devised platform takes from labor more than it gives.

The New Party, in this platform, pledges itself to social and industrial justice, and specifically to "work unceasingly for effective legislation looking to the prevention of occupational diseases, overwork, involuntary unemployment, and other injurious effects incident to modern industry," and it proceeds to set forth fourteen definite and distinct measures to that end.

But nowhere in that long and comprehensive platform, neither in its nobly-phrased statement of principles, not in its general recommendations, nor in its enumeration of specific measures, can there be found any pledge to secure the right of labor to organize, without which all other grants and concessions for improvement of the condition of the workingman are futile. It contains merely a friendly approval of the practice.

The platform promises social and industrial justice, but it does not promise industrial democracy.

The justice which it offers is that which the benevolent and wise corporation is prone to administer through its welfare department. There is no promise of that justice which free American workingmen striving to secure for themselves through organization. Indeed, the industrial policy advocated by the New Party would result in the denial of labor's right to organize.

The New Party stands for the perpetuation and the extension of private monopoly in industry—that private monopoly from which the few have ever profited at the expense of the many, and for the dethronement of which the people have, in the past, fought so many valiant battles.

That cursed product of despotism, the New Party, proposes to domesticate in our Republic, proclaiming: "We do not fear commercial power."

*Certainly, organized labor has had experience with the great trusts which should teach all men that commercial power may be so great that it is the part of wisdom to fear it.*

Great trusts—the Steel Trust, the Sugar Trust, the Beef Trust, the Tobacco Trust, the Smelter Trust—and a whole troop of lesser trusts—have made the extermination of organized labor from their factories the very foundation stone of their labor policy. *The ability to defeat labor's right to combine seems to have been regarded by the trust magnates as a proper test of the efficiency of their capitalistic combination.* And, indeed, this ability of the great trusts to overcome the workingman has been confidently relied upon by the trust advocates as one of the great "Savings of Combination."

Gilbert H. Montague, describing the Savings of Combination says:

"By its preponderant influence in the business, the trust has an enormous advantage in its dealings with combined labor. In 1899 during the smelters' strike in Colorado, the American Smelting and Refining Company closed the mills in which the strikers had been employed and transferred the work to its other mills; the effect was immediately to break the strike. The United States Steel Corporation had similar success in 1901 with the Amalgamated Association of Iron and Steel Workers. In the renewed labor contracts between the association and the union mills of the American Sheet Steel Company, the association demanded that the scale be extended to all the mills of the company. This was refused, and on July 15th, 75,000 men quit work in the mills of the sheet steel, steel hoop, and tinplate companies. Had the association been dealing with competing employers, each eager to keep his mills running and to get the orders which his recalcitrant rivals could not accept, its demands would soon have been granted.

"During that same year, the members of the International Association of Machinists had played upon the mutual distrust of their employers and had obtained the nine-hour day. The United States Steel Corporation, however, with its solid resistance and its immense defense fund, filled its orders from other mills, and before fall completely broke the strike. When workmen are not entirely organized throughout an industry, the advantage of combination over smaller enterprise is of first importance."

The United States Steel trust was exceedingly prompt in introducing this economy. On June 17, 1901, six weeks after it began its operation, its executive committee passed this vote, which was offered by Charles Steele, a partner of George W. Perkins in the firm of J. P. Morgan & Company:

*"That we are unalterably opposed to any extension of union labor and advise subsidiary companies to take firm position when these questions come up and say that they are not going to recognize it, that is, any extension of union in mills where they do not now exist."*

You know the gallant fight which the unionists made. It was a long hard struggle. It meant for the union men and their families terrible sacrifices. The men fought well. The women and children suffered cheerfully, but defeat came; and it was inevitable. The union men were opposed to an irresistible force. The financial resources of the great trusts are inexhaustible; the best brains of the country are at their disposal; their organization is compact; their policy is stable, and the strikebreaker with all that power behind him is a potent force. The trust is immune even from the consequences of enforced suspension of work. For if you curtail its production, you do not necessarily injure the trust. Control of the market enables it to charge higher prices when production is lessened; it compensates itself for loss of product by the higher price and the consumer loses, not the trust. Against this huge power, organized labor with its loosely-banded, ill-provisioned forces necessarily battles in vain. So, it was inevitable that organized labor should lose the fight against the great steel trust.

You know what followed: The great bulk of American union laboring men in the iron and steel industry were made to understand that they were not wanted at the works of the United States Steel Corporation. Places once filled by American laborers loyal to their union were given to others; and, as the Stanley Committee found:

"Hordes of laborers from Southern Europe poured into the United States. They were almost entirely from the agricultural classes, knew absolutely nothing about iron and steel manufacture, but were sufficient to fight the labor unions. They were absolutely unskilled, but they could work, especially as common laborers. In times of special necessity even advertisements for foreign help of this class were spread broadcast." This is one of them:

"WANTED—*Sixty tin house men tinners, catchers, and helpers to work in open shops; Syrians, Poles, and Romanians preferred; steady employment and good wages to men willing to work; fare paid and no fees charged for this work. Central Employment Bureau, 628 Pennsylvania Avenue.*"

And as the Stanley Committee further found:

"The result is that about 80 per cent of the unskilled laborers in the iron and steel business are foreigners of these classes. With the benefit of a skilled American foreman such a crew can work out results in unskilled labor production. The profits of this system of labor employment go to the Steel Corporation, while the displaced American workman shifted as best he could."

But unionism, like Truth, "crushed to earth will rise again." Tyranny—industrial as well as political—can maintain itself only by coercion and repression. So, the immediate and continuing result of the Steel Trust's triumph over organized labor has been an extensive system of espionage and repression. Through detectives it has shadowed its own employees as if they were insidious enemies; and has picked off, one by one, any men in whom unionism was detected or suspected. As John Fitch, who testified before the Stanley Committee says:

"The fact is the steel workers do not dare openly express their convictions. They do not dare assemble and talk over affairs pertaining to their welfare as mill hands. They feel that they are living always in the presence of a hostile critic. They are a generous, open-hearted set of men upon the whole. The skilled men are intelligent and are able and glad to talk upon a variety of subjects. But let the conversation be shifted to the steel works and they immediately become reticent. It is safe to talk with a stranger about local option, the price of groceries, or the prospect of war with Japan, but it is not regarded as safe to talk about conditions in the steel industry."

Again, he says:

"One man of long experience as a steel worker who gave me a better insight into mill conditions than any other one person, remarked, 'I used to write for labor papers a great deal, and sometimes I fairly burn to do it now—to declare before the world, over my own signature, the facts about working conditions in the steel industry. But I can't. It wouldn't be safe.'"

That is free America—not despotic Russia.

Espionage and discharge as a trust method of subjugating labor is supplemented by the subtler and gentler device of "welfare work." The Steel Corporation has done much work of this character to be commended. Stung by the whip and scorn of publicity, this sensitive corporation has for several years made great strides in introducing safety appliances and during the last year has gone far in reducing the seven-day week; and it has provided compensation for accidents and established a pension system. But its compensation and pension schemes are so devised as to rob the detached workman of an all powerful corporation of what glimmer of freedom and independence remained. They create a new form of peonage.

The pension plan of the United States Steel Corporation which took effect January 1, 1911, provides pensions only for those who have been in the employ of the company at least twenty years, and remain until the time for retirement; but no one has the RIGHT TO REMAIN in the employ:

*Article 26*: "Neither the creation of this fund nor any other at any time taken by any corporation included under the provisions of the fund, or by the board of trustees, shall give to any employee the right to be retained in the service, and all employees remain subject to discharge to the same extent as if this pension fund had never been created."

Even if the worker has remained in the employ until the time fixed for retirement, and has served faithfully, he has no right to a pension:

*Article 24*: "The pension plan is a purely voluntary provision for the benefit of employees superannuated or totally incapacitated after long and faithful service and constitutes no contract and confers no legal rights upon any employee."

And a board of trustees, in whose selection the workers have no voice and on which they have no representation, may refuse to grant them a pension or may terminate it after it has been granted for what they, in their discretion, deem adequate cause:

*Article 22*: "Pensions may be withheld or terminated in case of misconduct on the part of the beneficiaries or for other cause sufficient in the judgment of the board of trustees to warrant such action."

It has often been said by the corporations that one of their purposes in establishing a pension system is to "develop loyalty." But provisions like those quoted above suggest a purpose rather to *compel* than to develop "loyalty." The system is in effect a form of strike insurance. The pension is made dependent upon continuity of employment for a fixed period. The worker cannot receive a pension unless he remains in the company's employ until the date for retirement, and he has no right to remain in its employ, since the company reserves the full power to discharge him at any time, with or without cause. After a wage earner has served a number of years and feels himself growing older, the prospect of a pension becomes a potent influence. He realizes that if he abandons his position or is discharged, he loses not only immediate employment, but protection for old age. He realizes also that the chance of securing other employment is greatly diminished by reason of his advancing years; diminished not because he is already old and less efficient, but because he will become superannuated sooner than a younger man, so that his employment by another concern will impose upon it or its pension system a superannuation burden sooner than if a younger man were selected.

Are not the features in the pension system like those quoted above designed to make the wage earner compliant? He can be more readily relied upon to prove "loyal" and not to "go out" even if others strike for higher wages and better working conditions. The "continuous employment feature" of the pension system tends thus to rivet the wage earner to his employer, and the provision by which the allowance of a pension is made discretionary further insures "loyalty" of the wage earner during his employment. An employee of the United Steel Corporation advancing in years might well be deterred from hazarding the prospect of a pension by trade union activity, or even by joining a union.

And the Accident Compensation Plan contains a provision of the same character which is even less defensible. It a man has been working less than five years for the Steel Corporation when he gets hurt he receives only 35 per cent of his weekly wages as compensation. After five years the amount of compensation increases 2 per cent for each year. Can that provision have any other purpose than to curtail the man's freedom to leave? What has the length of service to do properly with the amount one should receive as compensation for an injury? This same device for fastening the man to the company pervades the Steel Corporation's stock distribution plan, sometimes erroneously called "Profit Sharing."

Now, what has been the result of this labor policy of the Trust? Judge Gary, chairman of the world's greatest trust—the Steel Corporation—says:

"*I believe, taking everything into account, the treatment accorded by our corporation to its employees compares favorably with that of any kind of industry in this country, or in any other country at the present time or at any period in the history of the world.*"

His close associate, Mr. George W. Perkins, confirms Judge Gary's testimony; and Mr. Perkins's testimony is entitled to great consideration, because he not only has been Chairman of the Finance Committees of the Steel Trust and the Harvester Trust; but he is now, also, the Chairman of the Executive Committee of the New Party, and head of its Industrial Department. Mr. Perkins might almost be called the "Father of Trusts," because for many years, while partner in the firm of J. P. Morgan & Co., he was specially active in the organization of these industrial combinations. And his wide experience is not limited merely to promoting trusts. He has had an important part in carrying on the business of trusts after organization. He has been a director of the Steel Trust ever since it commenced business in 1901. He was Chairman of its Finance Committee when it took over the Tennessee Coal & Iron Company. He has been chairman of the Finance Committee of the Harvester Trust since its organization. He has been a director of the great Shipping Trust—the International Mercantile Marine—ever since its organization. He had also other wide business experience before these trusts were formed; having been Vice President of the New York Life Insurance Company in the golden days before Charles E. Hughes investigated the life insurance companies. He is now a defendant in the suits the government has brought for the dissolution of the Steel Trust and the Harvester Trust.

Now, Mr. Perkins and Judge Gary are, undoubtedly, experts on trusts; but the report of Chas. P. Neill, United States Commissioner of Labor, made last winter, shows that they are not experts on labor conditions: for instead of that labor paradise which Judge Gary describes Dr. Neill found this to be the condition of the steel and iron worker.

First: As to hours of labor.

"During May, 1910, the period covered by this investigation into the steel industry, 50,000 persons, or 20 per cent of the 153,000 employees of the blast furnaces, steel works, and rolling mills covered by this report, customarily worked seven days per week, and 20 per cent of them worked 84 hours or more a week, which, in effect, means a 12 hour working day every day in the week, including Sunday.

"This hardship of 12-hour day and 7-day week is still further increased by the fact that every week or two weeks, as the case may be, when the employees on the day shift are transferred to the night shift, and *vice versa*, employees remain on duty without relief either 18 or 24 consecutive hours, according to the practice adopted for the change of shifts. The most common plan to effect this change of shift is to work one shift of employees on the day of change through the entire 24 hours, the succeeding shift working the regular 12 hours when it comes on duty."

Second: As to wages.

There has been a tradition that the steel worker was highly paid. Once this was true. Formerly the percentage of skilled workers in the trade was large, and their pay was very high. Now the percentage of skilled workers is much smaller, and, though the cost of living has risen, skilled workers remaining are paid less than they formerly were. Of all the workers, nearly 65 per cent are common laborers; and their pay has been so low, that, according to the report of the Associated Charities of Pittsburgh, the aggregate wages which a man could earn in a year, if he worked 12 hours a day, 365 days in a year, would not be sufficient for the bare subsistence of a family consisting of husband, wife and three children living under decent conditions. To sustain such a family in Pittsburgh, the minimum requirement was found to be $768 a year, and, at the rate paid by the Steel Corporation, a man who worked 12 hours a day, 365 days in the year, would fall just $1.50 short of earning that minimum amount.

But, of course, no man could stand it to work twelve hours a day every day in the year, and a common laborer doesn't often have the chance—certainly not if he is a steel worker. For in spite of the assertion that trusts make for regularity of employment, the report of the recent Federal Immigration Commission shows that, with possibly the single exception of coal mining, the iron and steel men worked a smaller percentage of the time during the period reported on than those in any of the trades investigated. And that report showed another thing which is very instructive. It showed that the average annual income of all males over 18 was only $346. The amount so earned in the industry was less than the earning in any other of the trades investigated. The average income of male heads of families among the iron and steel workers was only $409. In no other of the trades investigated was it so low, with the single exception of the woolen industry. Mr. Perkins testified before the Senate Committee to the value of profit sharing as a solvent for labor trouble and urged it as a reason for legalizing trusts.

He stated that ordinary employers of labor were too selfish to introduce profit-sharing plans. But that the Trust stocks were so widely distributed that the holders would not be likely to interfere with the wisely generous plans of the Trust officials. Then he added:

"I do not think that the question between labor and capital is so much a question of whether a man is paid $1.50 or $1.60 a day, as it is whether he thinks that he is getting his proper proportion of what is being earned."

Now let us see what Mr. Perkins's idea is of a fair share. He told of how the Steel Trust had introduced a profit-sharing plan, and distributed since it was organized $12,000,000 among its employees. As a matter of fact, the workers received none of that $12,000,000. It was distributed among superintendents, foremen, and others in authority, and you know how much that aids the workingman. As the Steel Trust had then been in operation ten years, and the number of employees nearly 200,000, that $12,000,000, if it had been distributed equally would have given each man $6 a year, or 50 cents a month. That, apparently, was Mr. Perkins's idea of a "fair share" for labor. He did not give the Committee his idea of what would be a fair share for the capitalist. I will tell you: For a few weeks' work in organizing that Trust, Mr. Perkins's firm took a promotion fee of $12,500,000. Just $500,000 more than according to Mr. Perkins' testimony was distributed among the Steel Trust employees during the whole ten years. But $12,500,000 was only a part of the promotion fees. J. P. Morgan & Co. got that amount for their own services as "Syndicate Managers." Another $50,000,000 was divided among themselves and other syndicate members. And they had gotten besides, shortly before, large sums for organizing several of the subsidiary companies of the Steel Trust. For only one of them, the National Hoop Company, the promotion fee was $20,000,000; that is, one-fourth of the $80,000,000 stock of the Company. These were merely the fees of the promoters which the financiers received. During the same period in which much labor was worked 84 hours a week or was paid starvation wages, there was, as the Commissioner of Labor found, paid out to stockholders, or accumulated for their benefit, more than $600,000,000 in excess of a fair return upon the actual value of the assets of the Company at time of organization.

Many of the New Party leaders admit such hardship to labor and such injustice as I have described. They grieve over it and want to put an end to such practices. They say it is because of these abuses that they advocate the policy of legalizing private monopoly and regulating it: or, in other words, domesticating industrial monsters and taming them. They propose to secure relief by legislation and an Interstate Trade Commission. *I, also, want legislation, and an Interstate Trade Commission to help enforce the laws; but I don't think the community ought to be forced or bribed into legalizing private monopoly in order to get the legislation and the Commission.* And it seems to me very unwise, particularly for labor, to surrender industrial liberty and to rely wholly upon legislation and a Commission. Legislation and Commissions help only "him who helps himself;" and a social program which accepts these things as a substitute for industrial liberty, instead of using them as means of securing industrial liberty, is fundamentally unsound. You know perfectly well that no legislation—even when sustained by the Court—and no Commission, though able and honest, will effectually protect labor, *unless the workingmen and public opinion are behind them.* For effective action there must be men behind legislation and Commissions, as well as behind guns; and the individual workingman is powerless. Numbers and unity of purpose are essential. Unless the right to organize is preserved and developed, all the laws advocated in the New Party platform, even if upheld by the courts, would be little better than dead letters.

But would these proposed laws be sustained by the courts?

Last month the New York Investigating Commission revealed the shocking conditions of the working women in the twine mills at Auburn belonging to another of Mr. Perkins' trusts—the International Harvester

Company. It showed that many of the girls and women received only $5 a week, and under the piece-work system could rarely earn more than $7. Many worked all night and lugged heavy burdens.

Mr. Perkins, being interviewed, said:

"The platform of the Progressive Party is strong on this very point declaring for a minimum wage and the prohibition of night work for women, and an 8-hour law."

Now, you have had some experience with 8-hour and other laws. It is hard to get them passed. It has proved hard indeed to have them sustained by the courts. It is harder to have them enforced than to get them enacted.

But would these laws which Mr. Perkins and the New Party platform propose be sustained by the courts?

The proposed laws legalizing private monopoly would doubtless be held constitutional, but how about the labor laws?

*First*: No compulsory minimum wage law, even for women, has yet been passed in America. It is uncertain whether any courts (except Ohio, under the recent constitutional amendment) would hold it constitutional. It is practically certain that the New York courts would hold it invalid.

*Second*: No American court has yet held that a law prohibiting night work for women is valid. There has been but one decision in the United States involving such a law. That was rendered by the Court of Appeals of New York, and it has already declared the law unconstitutional.

*Third*: No American court has yet held a general law limiting the hours of labor in private industry, constitutional. The Supreme Court of the United States, and some state courts have held such a law valid when applied to women. Many courts have held 8 hours laws valid for both men and women in public employment or where in private business there was special danger to health or safety. But so far, the courts have insisted that the legislature had ordinarily no power to limit the hours of labor for men; and the Supreme Court of the United States held this to be the law in the bakers' case arising under a New York statute. Of course, federal and state constitutions might be changed so as to make any such laws constitutional; and in my opinion they should be so changed without delay. But wouldn't it be safer not to legalize monopoly and facilitate the extermination of unionism from the great industries until the constitutions are so amended? If the trust magnates get their trusts legalized now through the New Party so that the financiers can market their watered stock with the label "Guaranteed under the Government Pure Investment Act," these gentlemen can patiently await the slow march of constitutional amendments, legislation and court decision. And they may so wait in comfortable reliance upon the fact that until the Federal Constitution is so amended neither Congress, nor the Interstate Trade Commission can prevent their discharging employees for joining trade unions; because the Supreme Court of the United States, in the Adair case, only a few years ago held that Congress was powerless to interfere because a corporation engaged in inter-state commerce has the constitutional right to discharge an American citizen from its employ for joining a labor union.

In view of these facts can workingmen safely vote for the New Party?

4

# Efficiency and the Trusts I

*There are two speeches in this book titled "Efficiency and the Trusts." Brandeis was an advocate of efficiency and in this speech, he makes the argument that trusts are inimical not just because of their high cost to consumers but also because they are even more inefficient than competition. This speech was given to the Town Criers in Providence, Rhode Island, on October 7, 1912. A typescript of the speech is held in folder NMF 50-1 of the Brandeis collection at the University of Louisville. It does not appear to have been published before.*

Efficiency is the supreme law to which all human institutions must ultimately bow. Occasionally inefficiency seems to enjoy success; but it is seeming merely. We are soon undeceived. We find that what seemed success was but a passing glow; or that we failed to apply the proper tests of success.

So, we may rest assured that the present great issue in America—the Trust Problem—will ultimately be decided in accordance with the demands of efficiency. Our care need be merely that we have the proper conception of efficiency; and that we be not misled by superficial and temporary indications of achievement.

Now, what is the proper test of efficiency in American industry? Before answering that question, consider for a moment how large a part business plays in American life. It would be but little exaggeration to say that: "Today business, in its larger sense, is life." Business probably occupies in America at present more of the thought and energy of a whole people than it ever did before, at any time, in any country in the history of the world. Not only has business become far more intense and pervasive in the field formerly occupied by it; but the realm of business has been vastly extended through organization and the advance of science, including as it now does, agriculture and many of the professions. And it reaches also a much larger percentage of the whole people, mainly, perhaps, because business has displaced much of women's domestic work; and women have in turn invaded industry. This fact—that business has become so large a part of life—makes it the more important to bear in mind while testing efficiency that business was made for man, not man for business. And to bear also in mind what America's aspirations are:

They are, for each and every citizen, liberty and equality of opportunity, including the opportunity for the full development of the best that is in the individual man.

Approaching the trust problem on this plane, let us inquire whether the trust can satisfy this social economic test of efficiency.

It will be found, I believe, that private monopoly is inefficient economically because (1) it tends rather to increase than decrease costs; (2) it tends rather to lessen than better quality; (3) it tends to arrest progress; [and] (4) it denies to the community the fruits of efficiency where it is attained. [Private monopoly is inefficient] socially because (1) it suppresses individual development; (2) it suppresses individual liberty and defeats social justice; [and] (3) it creates gross inequalities of power inconsistent with democratic institutions.

Let us understand first what the term "monopoly," as here used, means. A monopoly does not mean necessarily a concern which does all the business in a particular line. Even the Shoe Machinery Trust doesn't quite accomplish that. It means a concern which controls the market—as the Standard Oil, or the Tobacco Trust, or the Steel Trust [did] before the Stanley investigation. On the other hand, an independent or competitive concern does not mean necessarily a small or ill-equipped concern. The Carnegie Company before the Steel Trust was formed [and] the McCormick Company before the Harvester Trust was formed, were independent; but they were not small concerns or ill-equipped.

Earnest argument is constantly made in support of monopoly by pointing to the wastefulness of competition. Undoubtedly competition involves waste. What human activity does not? The wastes of democracy are among the greatest obvious wastes, but we have compensations in democracy which far outweigh that waste and make it more efficient than absolutism. So it is with competition. Incentive and development which are incidents to the freer system of business result in so much greater achievement that the waste is relatively insignificant. The margin between that which men naturally do, and that which they can do is so great that a system which urges men on to action and develops individual enterprise and initiative is preferable, in spite of the wastes that necessarily attend that process. I say necessarily, because there have been and are today wastes incidental to competition, that are unnecessary, the wastes of competition which do not develop, but kill. That waste the law can and should eliminate, by regulating competition, and to that end, among others, the provisions of the LaFollette-Stanley Anti-Trust bills were directed.

Efficiency does not necessarily increase with size. It is, of course, true that the unit in business may be too small to be efficient. The larger unit has been a common incident of monopoly. But a unit too small for efficiency is by no means a necessary incident of competition. It is also true that the unit in business may be too large to be efficient, and this is no uncommon incident of monopoly. In every business concern there must be a size limit of greatest efficiency. What that limit is will differ in different businesses and under varying conditions in the same business. But whatever the business or organization, there is a point where it would become too large for efficient and economic management, just as there is a point where it would be too small to be an efficient instrument. The limit of efficient size is exceeded when the disadvantages attendant upon size outweigh the advantages, when the centrifugal force exceeds the centripetal. Man's work often outruns the capacity of the individual man; and, no matter what the organization, the capacity of an individual man usually determines the success or failure of a particular enterprise, not only financially to the owners, but in service to the community. Organization can do much to make concerns more efficient. Organization can do much to make larger units possible and profitable. But the efficiency even of organization has its bounds; and organization can never supply the combined judgment, initiative, enterprise, and authority which must come from the chief executive officers. Nature sets a limit to their possible accomplishment. As the Germans say: "Care is taken that the trees do not scrape the skies."

That mere size does not bring success is illustrated by the records of our industrial trusts during the past ten years. This record, if examined, will show that:

(1) Most of the trusts which did not secure monopolistic positions have failed to show marked success as compared with the independent concerns.

This is true of many existing trusts; for instance, of the Newspaper Trust, the Writing Paper Trust, the Upper Leather Trust, the Sole Leather Trust, the Woolen Trust, the Paper Bag Trust, the International Mercantile Marine; and those which have failed, like the Cordage Trust, the Mucilage Trust, the Flour Trust, should not be forgotten.

(2) Most of those trusts which have shown marked success secured monopolistic positions either by controlling the whole business themselves, or by doing so in combination with others. And their success has been due mainly to their ability to fix prices.

This is true, for instance, of the Standard Oil Trust, the Shoe Machinery Trust, the Tobacco Trust, the Steel Trust, and the Pullman Car Company.

(3) Most of the trusts which did not secure for themselves monopoly in their particular branch of trade but controlled the situation only through price agreements with competitors, have been unable to hold their own share of the market as against the independents.

This is true, for instance, of the Sugar Trust, the Steel Trust, and the Rubber Trust.

(4) Most of the efficiently managed trusts have found it necessary to limit the size of their own units for production and for distribution.

This is true, for instance, of the Tobacco Trust, the Standard Oil Truest, and the Steel Trust.

These general rules are of course subject to exceptions due to instances of conspicuous ability on the part of managers or unusual trade conditions.

Of course, there are monopolies which are efficiently managed and competitive concerns which are very inefficiently managed; but it will be found that on the whole monopolies tend, in the long run, to increase rather than decrease the cost of production and distribution and to deteriorate rather than improve quality.

But the efficiency of monopolies, even if established, would not justify their existence unless the community should reap benefit from the efficiency; and experience teaches us that whenever trusts have developed efficiency, their fruits have been absorbed almost wholly by the trusts themselves. From such efficiency as they have developed the community has gained substantially nothing. For instance:

The Standard Oil Trust, an efficiently managed monopoly, increased the prices of its principal products (refined oil, naphtha and paraffin wax) between 1895 and 1898, and 1903 to 1906 by 46 per cent. The profits per gallon on crude oil used increased from 1882 to 1906 from 1.78 per gallon to 3.05 per gallon. The profits of the marketing companies of the Trust increased from .88 cents per gallon of illuminating oil in 1898 to 1.50 cents per gallon in 1906. The profits on naphtha per gallon nearly doubled between 1898 and 1906.

The Tobacco Trust, an efficiently managed monopoly. Between 1899 and 1907 the selling price (less taxes) on smoking tobacco rose from 21.1 cents per pound to 30.1 cents; the profit per pound from 2.8 cents per pound to 9.8 cents. The selling price of plug tobacco rose from 24.9 cents per pound to 30.4 cents; the profit per pound from 1.9 cents to 8.7 cents.

In the snuff business the Tobacco Trust controlled 96 per cent of the market. The extortion was even greater. The selling price of snuff (less taxes) rose from 29.2 cents per pound in 1900 to 37.1 cents in 1907; whereas the cost decreased from 22.6 cents per pound to 20.8 cents. Thus, the profit per pound exacted by the Trust rose from 6.6 cents per pound to 16.3 cents per pound. In other words, in 1907 on every pound of snuff sold by the Trust was exacted from the public a profit of about 81 per cent on its cost.

The following statement of the Commissioner of Corporations illustrated the power and disposition of the trust to absorb whatever profits existed:

"The results of the Spanish War tax upon tobacco products especially illustrate the monopolistic power of the Combination. When that tax was imposed in 1898, prices were generally raised. In 1901 and 1902 the tax was reduced to its former basis, but the Combination was powerful enough to keep its prices at the higher level. It thus absorbed practically all the benefit of the reduction, adding millions yearly to its income. The episode shows the unforeseen results of fiscal legislation affecting monopolistic conditions not fully recognized. The tax reduction, of course, was intended to benefit the consumers. As a matter of fact, it benefited almost solely the controlling interest in the industry."

The Steel Trust, a corporation of reputed efficiency. The high prices maintained by it in the industry are matters of common knowledge. In less than ten years it accumulated for its shareholders or paid out as dividends on stock representing merely water, over $650,000,000.

Compare with this record of increased or stationary prices and of growing profits, the record of strictly competitive manufacturing businesses, where the selling prices have shown a marked tendency to decrease and the ratio of profits has been almost uniformly lessened.

For instance, the book paper business furnishes a conspicuous example of this. In important mills, the average selling price of book paper declined from 7.08 cents per pound in 1889 to 4.24 cents in 1899, and to 3.99 in 1910; the ratio of profit per pound declined from 19 per cent on cost in 1889 to 13 per cent in 1899 and 7 per cent in 1910. This reduction is the more noteworthy because the principal raw material used—wood—(like wages) has steadily risen in price during the period.

The proposed Government Commission to fix prices would not greatly relieve the evils attendant upon monopoly. It might be effective in preventing private monopoly from taking excessive profits. But government price regulation would be powerless to secure to the public the low prices commonly attendant upon competition. In other words, price fixing might reduce the trust's profits, but it would fail to materially reduce the trust's prices; because the limitation of the monopoly's profits would, by lessening this incentive, surely reduce the monopoly's efficiency.

Capital and property will yield according to the degree of the judgment and efficiency applied in management vastly different returns. To secure the successful management of any private business reward must be proportionate to success. The establishment of any rule fixing a maximum return on capital would, by placing a limit upon the fruits of achievement, tend to lessen efficiency. For efficiency is naturally reflected in large net earnings; and as no ready means exists for determining whether greater net earnings are due to greater efficiency in management or to excessive profits, large net earnings would be followed by compulsory reduction of prices, and such reduction by a lessening of effort. To take from a private business the natural fruits of efficiency would create a sense of injustice suffered, which would paralyze effort and individual enterprise, and produce slipshod management. The attempt to secure low prices through price fixing would prove as impotent as the statutes which have sought to protect the public in respect to railroad rates by limiting the dividends of railroads. The permissible dividends generally exhausted the profits. No selling price for monopoly products could be set constitutionally at a point lower than that which would allow a reasonable return on capital. And in the absence of comparative data from any competing businesses producing the same article at less cost it would be practically impossible to determine that the cost should be lower.

And more serious and more insidious even than the tendency to increase cost or to reduce quality is monopoly's deadly arrest of progress in the trade which it controls. As the memorial transmitted last year by the "Inventors Guild" to the President declared:

"It is a well-known fact that modern trade combinations tend strongly toward constancy of process and products, and by their very nature are opposed to new processes and new products originated by independent inventors, and hence tend to restrain competition in the development and sale of patents and patent rights; and consequently tend to discourage independent inventive thought, to the great detriment of the Nation, and with injustice to inventors whom the Constitution especially intended to encourage and protect in their rights."

And this recital is confirmed by the editorial statement in the *Engineering News*—a high authority—which declared last year:

"We are today something like five years behind Germany in iron and steel metallurgy, and such innovations as are being introduced by our iron and steel manufacturers are most of them merely following the lead set by foreigners years ago.

"We do not believe this is because American engineers are any less ingenious or original than those of Europe, though they may indeed be deficient in training and scientific education compared with those of Germany. We believe the main cause is the wholesale consolidation which has taken place in American industry. A huge organization is too clumsy to take up the development of an original idea. With the market closely controlled and certain profits by following standard methods, those who control our trusts do not want the bother of developing anything new.

"We instance metallurgy only by way of illustration. There are plenty of other fields of industry where exactly the same condition exists. We are building the same machines and using the same methods as a dozen years ago, and the real advances in the art are being made by European inventors and manufacturers."

Monopoly's tendency to stifle the development of the individual manifests itself in every department of business activity. In the executives, as well as the inventors—in the highest official as well as among the lowliest workmen, the scientist would have less difficulty in detecting the germ of Monopolitis, than they did the effect of the hookworm.

A lawyer—who has gained national prominence as a trust builder, but believes thoroughly in competition—said to me recently:

"The trusts have to an increasing extent encroached upon the field of American industry for nearly a generation; but you can't name me a single captain of industry developed by the trusts. *Captains of industry can make trusts; but trusts can't make captains of industry.*"

Trusts are not even made mainly by captains of industry. They are the creatures of, and marking, the coming of the money kings.

I thought over this lawyer's statement a long time, but I couldn't disprove it. Can you?

The Oil Trust had been in existence thirty-three years. When you think of the oil business you think of Rockefeller, Flagler, Pratt, Archbold and Rogers—all builders of the Trusts. Has the trust developed in a generation a single man of such conspicuous ability as to be a national character?

The Tobacco Trust had been in existence twenty years. When you think of the Tobacco Trust you think of Duke, Lorrilard, Drummond, Ligget and Meyers, Allen and Ginter. They are all men who built the trust or were absorbed by it. There is not a single name prominent in the tobacco world which the trust has developed. Thomas Fortune Ryan and [the manuscript is blank at this point] are widely known in connection with the Tobacco Trust, not as captains of industry, but as financiers; and as such they became trust builders.

In the Steel industry you still think of Carnegie and Frick and Schwab as the real captains, unless it be Judge Gary and George W. Perkins, who are, of course, conspicuous as builders of trusts and not of an industry.

In the Beef industry you think only of the great trust builders, like Armour, Swift and Morris.

Cyrus McCormick, a builder of the Harvester Trust, still leads in that industry.

Sydney W. Winslow, the builder of the Shoe Machinery Trust, still occupies so completely the field in his business that he might almost be described as the Shoe Machinery Trust.

Since monopoly has this deadening effect upon those high in command, it is natural that it should depress the faculties of the underlings.

Mr. H. A. Holder, of Lynn, in a very thoughtful pamphlet entitled *Trusts, Business and Us,* endeavors to express the effect of trusts on man in the middle station:

"My complaint is not financial. My complaint is that I have not had, under recent conditions, a fair chance at the opportunities I have so far spent my life to fit myself to take.

"What I object to is what people fight for. Their liberty, their opportunity for full development. Their right to hand down their birthright to their children protected, strengthened, and made more valuable. Their right to the profits of their labor. In other words, their freedom and their independence, and the class I represent can fight for this.

"The trust of the past, as I see it, represents but one thing. Money as a power by its mere bulk exerted to crush out competition of individual effort. I appreciate that this definition may be perhaps criticized as too strong for the trust as so far developed but I maintain it is a fair one and only anticipates the absolute actual condition by a few years. The only reason that it is not absolutely true up to this time is not that it is not the necessary, logical, inevitable result of such conditions as it creates, but because the control of it was in the hands of very strong individualities in the shape of the men at the helm of the ship.

"Men, not the result of the trusts themselves, or of any type that the trusts can produce, but men who were brought up and developed under individual, competitive conditions more fierce perhaps than the world has ever before seen. It is the result of the strong and commanding individuality of these men that the conduct of business by the trusts has in the harm that it has so far wrought been much more apparent and real against individuals than it has against the business and the interests of the country as a whole."

The industrial trust is making more and more marked the line of cleavage between capitalist and worker. It is intensifying in industry the evils of the absentee landlord, evils from which Ireland and other communities have long suffered. The many small stockholders in the large corporations stand in no actual relation with the great masses of workers who are toiling for them. Scattered as these small stockholders necessarily are, distant as most of them are from the place of business of the company; ignorant of the details of its management, they assume no responsibility for the conduct of the enterprise and regard it merely as an impersonal source of profit. The interests of their absent stockholders become necessarily allied closely with those in financial control. Their only care is the continuance or increase of the dividend, for ownership and responsibility are no longer combined. Already the industrial trusts are breeding all the social evils of absentee landlordism. An illustration of this is furnished by the Steel Trust's treatment of labor.

According to the report of the United States Commissioner of Corporations, Herbert Knox Smith, the United States Steel Corporation added to its assets in its first ten years $435,000,000 out of surplus earnings and paid out to stockholders during that period in dividends on stock which originally represented water only, over $222,000,000. In other words, this Company exacted from the public in ten years for its stockholders over $650,000,000 in excess of a fair return upon invested property.

What has it done for labor?

John Fitch's study of the steel workers of Pittsburgh supplies the answer:

"The formation of the United States Steel Corporation has brought more than fifty per cent of the steel workers of the country under one employer, with a result of uniformity of conditions of labor. Decisions from a single head, affect, without chance of protest, vast masses of men. In the course of stupendous changes in process and in corporate organization, unionism has been driven out of the mills of the Pittsburgh district. With its elimination has come an increase in hours until the 8 hour day has practically disappeared. The majority of employees engaged in processes of making steel work 12 hours. Many work seven days in the week, either without a full day of rest, or with a free Sunday one week, and 24 hours of continuous duty the next. Speeding up methods [has] augmented production in every department. Even where no new processes or machines have been introduced, the output has increased and in many cases is double what it was 15 years ago."

The increase in the hours and intensity of labor has in spite of the extraordinary earnings of the steel corporation not been attended by corresponding increase in wages. In some departments there have been increases, but less than the increase in the cost of living. In other departments there have been large decreases in spite of the increase in the cost of living.

Thus, Fitch states:

"As to the wages of the day laborers, in 1892 they received 14 cents an hour in Homestead; in 1907–8 their pay was 16 1/2 cents per hour in mills of the United States Steel Corporation, an advance of 18 per cent over the hourly pay of 1892. This increase fell short by 4 per cent in keeping pace with the increased cost of necessities, as indicated by the Bureau of Labor Bulletin."

[In regard to] the earnings of the crews in one place mill at Homestead in 1907 as compared with 1892, Fitch further states:

"The daily earnings of the men in the crews fell off from five to forty per cent. Had they continued on the 8 hour basis their loss must have been much greater than it was. As it was, they were not able, in spite of the increase in tonnage they handled, to maintain their old income, even by working 12 hours, in 1907, as against 8 hours in 1892, an increase in the working day of 50 per cent."

According to the report made by the Associated Charities in Pittsburg on the cost of living, a common laborer in the steel mills who worked 12 hours a day, 365 days in a year, would still fall $1.50 short of earning enough to support himself, wife and three children with a minimum of decency; and more than 60 per cent of all steel workers are common laborers.

This degradation of the condition of the laborer was made possible by driving out union labor. The underlying labor policy of the steel corporation is the determination "to control—in pursuance of which object the employers excluded the men from any voice in the conditions of their employment. Consistent with this policy repressive measures have been introduced, designed to enable the companies to retain the advantages which they gained for themselves when they eliminated the union. These measures were doubtless intended to preserve industrial efficiency, but they have resulted in a thorough going and far-reaching censorship that curtails free speech and free activity of citizens. The effect of these measures is seen in every department of community life, wherever in Allegheny County steel is made."

The destruction of unionism which renders possible such labor conditions has been a cardinal principle in the management of all of the powerful trusts: the Standard Oil Trust, the Tobacco Trust, the Shoe Machinery Trust, the Harvester Trust, the Cash Register Trust. The resulting conditions are inconsistent with democracy. They menace our institutions. They prevent the attainment of American ideals.

Industrial liberty must attend political liberty. America's lead in the industrial world is due more to the spirit and ability incident to a free people, than to its boundless resources. We have led the world industrially not so much because the resources of nature were unbounded, as because the faculties and aspirations of Americans were comparatively unfettered. We need, for the development of our industries, as for the development of our citizens, the highest degree of liberty attainable. Industrial democracy should ultimately attend political democracy. Industrial absolutism is undesirable and should be impossible. We must avoid industrial despotism, even though it be benevolent despotism. Our employers can no more afford to be absolute masters of their employees than they can afford to submit to the mastery of their employees. Neither should feel that he stand in the power—at the mercy—of the other. The sense of unrestricted power is just as demoralizing for the employer as it is for the employee. Neither our intelligence, nor our characters, can long stand the strain of unrestricted power. Every business requires for its business health the *momento mori* of competition from without. It requires likewise a certain competition from within, which can exist only where the ownership and management on the one hand, and the employees on the other, shall each be alert, hopeful, self-respecting, and free to work out for themselves the best conceivable condition.

The successful, the powerful trusts, have created conditions absolutely inconsistent with these—America's—industrial and social needs. It may be true that as a legal proposition mere size is not a crime, but mere size may become an industrial and social menace, because it frequently creates as against possible competitors and as against the employees, conditions of such gross inequality as to imperil the welfare of the employee and of the industry.

Since private monopoly is not beneficial to the community there can remain but two questions:

First: Can we preserve competition where it exists?

Second: Can we restore competition where it has been suppressed?

To both questions the answer is yes.

Diagnosis shows monopoly to be an artificial, not natural, product. Competition, therefore, may be preserved by preventing that course of conduct by which, in the past, monopolies have been established. If we had in the past, undertaken by appropriation legal and administrative machinery to prevent our financiers and others from carrying out agreements to form monopolies; if we had seriously attempted to prevent those methods of destructive or unfair competition, as are manifest in "cut-throat" competition—discrimination against customers who will not deal exclusively with the combination; if we had made any persistent intelligent effort to stop advantages gained by railroad discrimination; espionage, or the practice of establishing "fake independents"; or to stop those who have secured control of essential raw material from denying business rivals access to it, few of the trusts, of which we now complain, would have come into existence—or would at all events, have acquired power to control the market. We made no serious attempt to stop monopoly—certainly no intelligent attempt; partly because we lacked knowledge, partly because we lacked desire; for we had a sneaking feeling that perhaps after all a private monopoly might be a good thing, and we had no adequate governmental machinery to employ for this purpose. But in the past twenty-two years we have acquired much experience with trusts. We know their ways. We have learned what the defects in the existing machinery are; and if we will but remedy those defects by appropriate legal and administrative machinery, somewhat on the lines proposed in the La Follette-Stanley and Newlands bills, and supplement the prohibition of monopoly by the regulation of competition, we shall be able, not only to preserve the competition we now enjoy, but gradually regain the free soil upon which private monopoly has encroached, and we may be assured that, despite all industrial changes, the day for industrial liberty has not yet passed.

5

# Efficiency and the Trusts II

*The efficiency in this speech refers to the laws regulating trusts, specifically the Sherman Act. This speech was given to the Cleveland Chamber of Commerce on October 15, 1912, and was published in the January 22, 1913, issue of* The Fuel Magazine.

Recent criminal manifestations in a number of large American cities do not mean to my mind that our people are inferior to what they have been, or less desirous of attaining the ideals which were set before the American people. They mean that in some way respect for law, confidence in law as the means of attaining justice and right, no longer prevails to the degree essential to the welfare of our country. It behooves us, coming together at this time, to consider why it is that respect for law, the very basis of our government, is apparently waning throughout the country and is subjecting us in a single year to such conditions as these.

This waning respect for law is due to the fact that our law, as it has been practiced and as it has been written, is not fully deserving of respect, and if we desire to reinstate respect for law in this country, we must make the law itself respectable. Law is not respected for two reasons—because the law, as administered, does not fully express the will of the American people, and that the clearly expressed will of the American people is not carried out because of the inefficiency in the law itself. And for the latter defect I regret to say that my own profession is in large part responsible.

I came here to speak to you on the subject of trusts, and I know no subject which better illustrates this lack of respect for law, and the inefficiency of legal procedure. Everybody agrees that we need some new legislation. On the one hand, there is the general demand that abuses incident to trusts, which have manifested themselves in recent years, be eliminated. On the other hand, there is the demand of legitimate business for a settlement of problems which seriously disturb it. The question before us is, what line of action shall we pursue? On the one hand, we are urged to admit monopoly, to legalize the trust and to regulate it; on the other, we are urged to preserve competition, to restore it where it has been suppressed, and to regulate competition in order that it may be preserved.

Those who do ask that the trusts be legalized do so largely because as they point out that for twenty-two years trusts have flourished, and the Sherman law has been practically a dead letter. They point to the lamentable failure of the recent proceedings against the oil trust and the tobacco trust as evidence that trusts are inevitable, that we cannot carry out the policy of competition, which was laid down twenty-two years ago, and that therefore we should bow to the so-called inevitable—legalize the trust, and undertake by skillfully devised machinery to remove those special abuses of which complaint has been made. See, gentlemen, what that contention involves. Pass for a moment the question which I wish to discuss with you later, whether the trust is desirable, whether it is efficient, economically and socially; pass that by for a moment and take the argument which you hear most: "that the trust is inevitable, that we cannot prevent combination," and see where this leads us with respect to this very fundamental inquiry of preserving respect for the law.

Twenty-two years ago, after the most careful consideration by Congress, a law was passed which declared that it was the economic policy of America that competition should be preserved. And in the face of that law, remaining unamended on the books, combinations developed which have encroached, year after year, very far upon the field of competitive industry. See what the effect would be upon the American people to find that the great and powerful financial interests of this country can go forward year after year and disregard the declared policy of this country, proceed to disregard it so far that in 1912 a political party and a large number of people standing for the best interests of America come forward and declare, "Let us legalize the trust, let us legalize that which under existing law has grown up illegally, because it is impossible, or possibly undesirable, to prevent private monopoly."

If that position, gentlemen, became the accepted policy of America, we would declare in substance that not only vested rights, but vested wrongs were to be supreme in this country. And there could be nothing to my mind which would so threaten the welfare of America and imperil everything that we are working for, which we prize today, as the solemn declaration of the inability of this government to carry out the will which the people have registered in an act of Congress. But failure to enforce the Sherman law has not been inevitable. It has been due, on the one hand, to the unwillingness to enforce it on the part of those having the power and charged with the duty. And it has been due to a very much greater extent to the fact that while the Sherman law declared our economic policy, it provided no adequate means for enforcing it. As the courts have applied the act, it was a declaration of an economic principle rather than a legally effective statute. And the ability of the great American lawyers in most parts of this country has for twenty odd years been devoted to nullifying the will of the people as expressed in that law, instead of trying to find ways of enforcing it.

Take this situation as it is being discussed today and as it has unfolded itself before the American people within twelve months, the failure of the proceedings against the Standard Oil and the tobacco trusts. To what are they due? Take the first, the feature to which everybody points: that although the Supreme Court, in a unanimous decision upon practically admitted facts, declared that competition should be restored, and divided these companies into parts, no real competition has come. Why? The case of the tobacco trust presents the matter in a simple form. In its alleged disintegration, the greater part of all the tobacco company's property was, with the approval of the court, divided among three companies, which it was intended should compete with one another. And what did the court do? It authorized a plan of so-called disintegration, by which these three companies should be owned by precisely the same persons in the same proportions. Could there by dint of greatest effort have been devised any method better calculated to prevent competition between the three companies than just that which was adopted? And wouldn't it have been perfectly simple for the court to have declared, "We insist that this property shall be divided among three companies in such way that no person who owns stock in one of those companies shall own stock in either of the other two companies, for, say, five years, until conditions of reasonable competition shall have been re-established." If a man had died leaving three parcels of real estate, and leaving three sons to inherit it, each son would have been tenant in common with the others in each of those three parcels, and any one of those sons could have come to the court and said, "Partition this property; give me one of the parcels, give my brother A another, and my brother B the third, and we will make up as between us in cash whatever differences in value are found to exist between the three properties." With that common precedent before the court, a precedent acted upon for centuries by the courts, a twentieth century court of equity nevertheless adopted in the Tobacco Company disintegration, as it adopted in respect of the Oil Company's disintegration, a method by which each fragment company was to be owned by the same persons in the same proportions. Wouldn't it have been surprising if the owners had competed against themselves?

Now, what is the other great failure incident to the disintegration of those trusts? It is this: the Supreme Court, upon a most voluminous record, recounting the history of these companies, testified to copiously by those who were the victims of the effort to obtain monopoly, found that the great fortunes which had been gathered together in these companies were in large part the result of certain practices which everyone would recognize as being unfair and unsocial, and which ought to be, as they are, illegal. The report of the Commissioner of Corporations says in substance: "These huge fortunes, which have sent up to four and five and even to ten times the par value, stock which was originally represented largely by water, were not attained through superior efficiency; they were attained through practices recognized as being illegal and improper, among others largely railroad rebates." And yet, when the formal decree is entered, the court does nothing more than utter a futile, "Don't do it again." None of those witnesses who have appeared to bring the facts of their experience before the court, and set forth the record of their own destruction, not one of those is given any redress for the grave wrongs they have suffered. None of those who through extortionate prices was compelled to pay huge amounts to which the trust was not legally entitled, can recover anything.

That is the scandal to our legal system which has been discussed throughout the country. It has brought disrespect upon the law. It has made the poor man believe that it is only against him that the law is efficient. But was that result a necessary one? Certainly not. It is due to a rule of law that reads about thus: Though the government of the United States brings a proceeding against the trust for the benefit of 90-odd millions of people, and obtains a decree establishing all of its contentions, not one of those ninety millions of people is to be allowed to have individually any benefit of the proceeding brought on his behalf. If A or B or C, who have been crushed by the tobacco trust, wish to recover damages for that illegal act, they are obliged to proceed exactly as if the government had never acted; and as a matter of fact, if they did begin a proceeding or had undertaken to begin it a year ago, after those decrees were rendered, they would probably have been met by the bar that the statute of limitations had been running diligently against them while the government proceeding was pending. A person seeking damages from the Standard Oil Company for injuries resulting from the illegal combination would be obliged to prove again every fact which the government proved, so far as they might be deemed essential by the court; and it took twenty-four printed volumes of testimony to bring together all the evidence deemed necessary for the proper consideration of this question by the Supreme Court. Is there anything in the nation's inefficiency that could compare with that?

And see how easily that could be remedied by a line in the statute declaring that when the government had brought its proceeding and reached a decree declaring a combination to be illegal, then anyone who had been injured could bring his petition in that court, and by simply proving his damages could recover for his injury, and he would also not only recover merely the compensation for the damages suffered, because, you will find in the Sherman Act of twenty-two years ago the provision that a man who is injured shall recover not only the amount of damages suffered, but triple damages; and in order that he may be sure to be recompensed the law provides he should receive triple damages and in addition a reasonable counsel's fee. That provision in the act has been absolutely futile because of the rule to which I referred, that although the government proceeded on behalf of the people, not one of the people can have the benefit of that proceeding to redress the injury actually suffered by him.

Now, gentlemen, these are but two of the existing inefficiencies in our law in dealing with trusts, but the measures suggested show you how our law could be made efficient. And if you will read the La Follette–Lenroot bill or the Stanley bill, you will find in addition to those half a dozen other provisions which in one way or another would give vitality to that law and make that law as effective to carry out its work as any machine in your factory. Our law has lacked legal invention. We have been trifling with the people. We have been enacting statutes which purport to express the people's will and have left the laws ineffective. Jeeringly, jokingly, year after year, we have smiled over the inefficiency of that expression of the people's will, which there and elsewhere has gone upon the statute books to satisfy a popular demand.

It is, gentlemen, that sort of thing which is bringing on Los Angeles and Lawrence and Milwaukee incidents, and which if not corrected and corrected in the right manner will endanger all our institutions. To secure respect for our law, we must make the law respectable. We must increase the efficiency of our legal machinery, just as much as you in your factories must look out for efficiency. Otherwise, ruin will come upon you. Don't say we cannot enforce the law; particularly don't say so when it is the rich who are benefiting by the non-enforcement; or who will be believed to be benefiting by the non-enforcement. Do not legalize wrong done. The danger of such a course is too great and far-reaching.

I spoke of certain ways of perfecting and supplementing the Sherman law. There are others which are almost as necessary. We need a trade commission, an interstate or federal commission, which will undertake to see to it that law, whatever it may be, is observed. We need, besides the prosecuting attorney, the inspector and the policeman. We haven't that now. The fact that our anti-trust law has not been enforced does not prove that it is impossible to enforce its provisions. The fact proves rather that we have not put our will and minds to this task. If our lawyers and legislators had devoted to the problem of enforcing the law one one-hundredth part of the thought that they have devoted to defeating the will of the people as expressed in the Sherman law, we should have had today a commission which ascertained all important facts in regard to business, which undertook to see that those numerous practices which everyone condemns, which we all know about, and which are to so great an extent responsible for the growth of illegal monopoly, were made public; and the very publicity of them would go far toward eliminating them from actual practice; we should have had a commission protecting the individual merchant, as the Interstate Commerce Commission is protecting the individual shipper today. We should have had before this a knowledge of the real needs of business. We know much about the great trusts, but there is no adequate knowledge in the community in regard to that great multitude of questions involved in trade agreements between men in competitive business. In other words, we know about the trusts and monopolistic business, but we do not know about the trade agreements in competitive business; and we ought to have such knowledge. We ought to know to what extent such agreements are beneficial, and to what extent they are vicious; and until we know to what extent they are beneficent and to what extent they are vicious, we ought not to act concerning them. The trouble is that we have been undertaking to do in legislation that which every one of you would shrink from doing in your own business—we have been acting without possessing full knowledge of actual facts. In your business you go right to the facts, but a large part of legislation dealing with business has been based upon generalizations, upon feeling, upon wishes, rather than upon evidence. If we had such a trade commission and collected the necessary data concerning our business conditions, and duly considered such data we should eventually secure a law which would be wise and deserving of respect; and which, being deserving of respect, we might hope to enforce.

As I said before, people who urge the legalization of trusts, do it because they deem trusts inevitable; because they believe we cannot prevent their continued existence. But they also say that private monopoly may be, and often is, beneficial, and hence desirable. I believe that statement is also based upon generalization and without regard to actual facts; and without that careful investigation into the evidence and tendencies which is absolutely essential to correct judgment. Such an inquiry would prove that private monopoly, great capitalistic combinations, do not tend to economic efficiency, and that the success of them is temporary merely; that the great profits made were not earned through superior efficiency, but were secured through control of the market; were obtained practically through an exercise of the taxing power. Such an inquiry would disclose also that there inheres in those monopolies a great peril to American industry in the inevitable tendency, despite all effort of managers to the contrary, to deaden enterprise. One has only to look about this body and consider the great prosperity of Cleveland and of other American cities to learn whence our great successes have come. They have come through constant effort, through making men do more than the individual man ever thought he could do or ever would have done but for the pacemaker just beside him. Competition is attended by evils; but those evils so far as they result in what is destructive of property can be prevented by proper laws; in other words, by regulating competition. But the evil inherent in the deadening, stupefying effect of monopoly cannot be prevented by any regulation of monopoly. And those evils are not by any means evils merely dealing with the purely business side. Business was made for man, not man for business. And if we remember that business was made for man, we must not forget that any system under which business is to be done should be a system which will develop the individual man, and if there is any system which will develop the individual man better than the system of liberty, then we are wrong in our form of government. We ought to have a monarchy instead of a democracy, if it is better that we shall do for men than to let men do for themselves.

Nobody can value more than I do the important part which capital has played and must play in the development of our country. But, after all, gentlemen, if we are to attain real efficiency, economic and social, we must look forward to the time when men hire capital instead of capital hiring men. No system of scientific management, valuable as that system is, can ever bring out the possibilities in the individual man, without fine co-operation, and fine co-operation requires that the workers in the business—whether their positions be high or low—shall in effect be partners. That is, there must be co-operation not only in profits, but co-operation in action, in responsibility, in the exercise of power.

We in Boston are accustomed to looking to the Cleveland Chamber of Commerce as the parent organization of the Boston Chamber of Commerce. It was your inspiration which enabled us to form a businessman's organization worthy of our own city. And the man who brought that about, the man who brought us to the Cleveland idea and made that idea into a reality in Boston, was Edward A. Filene, one of the greatest social and economic thinkers in the country today. He is one of our ablest and most successful businessmen. It is only twenty-one years since the Filene brothers had two little stores in Boston, each about twenty feet square; one was a glove stand, the other a stand where they sold women's garments. Today these men are at the head of a business which occupies, in the very heart of our city, nine acres of floor space, and with sales of over ten millions a year. That financial success shows that the Filenes possess business ability of a high order. But those men have done much more for us; more for the whole country, than merely establishing a great business. They have recognized that business is a profession; and that there is a test of success in business better and finer than bulk or profits. They have recognized also to achieve success it is necessary that not only they, but all who are associated with them, should have the common spirit and the knowledge that that business is theirs in common. The Filene business today is essentially co-operative. Not only does one-half of the profit, after paying a fixed return upon capital, go to the ordinary worker, the other half going to the management, but every worker in that establishment has some part, or can have part in determining the rules under which he works, the condition under which he works. He can be heard by his own fellows as to his right to a promotion. He can be protected by his own fellows from discharge. Each has a reason to know that that business in essence is his business, in part, as it is the business of the other two thousand men and women who work in it. The Filenes and their associates are working out today real efficiency and industrial democracy. They are working out the problem which I believe is to be worked out in America, the problem of "Men controlling capital instead of capital controlling men." And the vital, conclusive argument against the real ultimate efficiency of the trusts, is that it is built upon the monarchic principle, the principle which must disappear from American industry, the principle that capital may hire men.

# 6

# The Regulation of Competition versus the Regulation of Monopoly

*This speech in which Brandeis outlines his solution to the trust problem was given to the Economic Club of New York on November 1, 1912. Parts of this speech were reprinted in the book* The Curse of Bigness, *but this is the first time the speech has been reprinted in its entirety since its initial publication in the 1913* Year Book of the Economic Club of New York. *Brandeis's call for an administrative board in this speech would help result in the creation of the Federal Trade Commission two years later. And in 2023, the FTC Chair Lina Khan would acknowledge Brandeis's speech in her own speech at the Economic Club.*

Ladies and Gentlemen: It is less than eighteen months since the decisions in the Standard Oil and tobacco cases made Americans realize the importance and the urgency of the trust problem. Since that time, there has been more intensive thought and serious discussion of the subject than during all the preceding twenty-one years which elapsed between the passage of the Sherman Act and the rendering of these decisions. And that thought, with general discussion, has been fruitful of results. It has not ripened into legislation; but it has done more. It has enlightened the American people and has brought the deliberations upon the subject to that stage where wise legislation is possible. The discussion has removed many misapprehensions which clouded the consideration of measures before the country. It has removed misconceptions also and has thus narrowed the field of controversy. A large part of the American people realize today that competition is in no sense inconsistent with large scale production and distribution. They realize that the maintenance of competition does not necessarily involve destructive and unrestricted competition, any more than the maintenance of liberty implies license or anarchy. We learned long ago that liberty could be preserved only by limiting in some way the freedom of action of individuals; that otherwise liberty would necessarily yield to absolutism; and in the same way, we have learned that unless there be regulation of competition, its excesses will lead to the destruction of competition, and monopoly will take its place.

A large part of our people have also learned that efficiency in business does not grow indefinitely with the size of business. Very often, a business grows in efficiency as it grows from a small business to a large business; but there is a unit of greatest efficiency in every business, at any time, and a business may be too large to be efficient, as well as too small. Our people have also learned to understand the true reason for a large of those huge profits which have made certain trusts conspicuous. They have learned that these profits are not due in the main to efficiency, but are due to the control of the market, to the exercise by a small body of men of the sovereign taxing power. Nothing has helped so much to make this clear to our people as an incident in the life of the tobacco trust. When the Spanish War came on and we needed additional revenue, Congress properly increased the tax on tobacco products; and then the trust very promptly raised the price of tobacco products. Three years later, when our country no longer needed that additional revenue, Congress sought to remove the burden which it had placed upon the people; but Congress found itself powerless to remove the burden it had imposed. And when Congress reduced the tax, the effect was merely to transfer, from the Treasury of the United States to the treasury of the trust, the several million dollars a year which represented the reduction in the tax; because the tobacco-products market was controlled by the trust, which held the selling price practically unchanged.

The history of the tobacco trust also showed in its detailed operations how control made for profit, for the degree of control exercised by that great trust was very different in the various departments of its business. And, as the Commissioner of Corporations found, the ratio of profit ordinarily was in direct relation to the ratio of control. Where the trust had a high degree of control, the profits were great; where they had a small degree of control, the profits were small. In the cigar business, in which the trust had no control of the market, in which it was merely a large concern, doing perhaps one-eighth of the cigar business of the country, the trust's profits were not only small, but they were very much smaller than would be satisfactory to the ordinary manufacturer. In the same year in which some of the subsidiary corporations of the trust were earning fifty, sixty, eighty, or one hundred per cent upon the tangible assets, the trust was earning in its cigar department only four to six per cent, although the ultimate management of all departments of the trust's business rested with the same able men and was supplied with the same great resources. Such facts as these have made men realize that while trusts are sometimes efficient, just as independent concerns are sometimes efficient, it is not their efficiency, but the fact that they control the markets, that accounts for the huge profits of trusts.

And people have learned also another fact of perhaps even greater importance. They have come to realize the effect of monopoly in arresting progress, arresting that advance in industry without which a great industrial future is unattainable.

Thirteen years ago, before combinations in the steel industry began, there was almost a panic in Europe at what they called "the American invasion." We had been making steel cheaper than any nation. Germany, Belgium, and England looked with alarm upon American competition. In 1911, twelve years after the era of combination in the steel industry began, the *Engineering News*, a high American authority, declared:

"We are today something like five years behind Germany in iron and steel metallurgy, and such innovations as are being introduced by our iron and steel manufacturers are most of them merely following the lead set by foreigners years ago. We do not believe that this is because American engineers are any less ingenious or original than those in Europe.... We believe the main cause is the wholesale consolidations which have taken place in American industry. A huge organization is too clumsy to take up the development of an original idea. With the market closely controlled, and profits certain by following standard methods, those who control our trusts do not want the bother of developing anything new. We instance metallurgy only by way of illustration. There are plenty of other fields of industry where exactly the same conditions exist. We are building the same machines and using the same methods as a dozen years ago, and the real advances in the arts are being made by European inventors and manufacturers."

That statement of the *Engineering News* was confirmed in a striking way in a memorial presented by the Inventors' Guild to the President last year. The memorial related specifically to the patent law, but it began with the recital of some facts, and this is one of the recitals:

"It is a well-known fact that modern trade combinations tend strongly toward constancy of prices and of products, and by their very nature are opposed to new processes and new products originated by independent inventors, and hence tend to restrain competition in the development and sale of patents and patent rights."

There you have it, the tendency of monopoly to arrest progress, the tendency of monopoly to standardize prices and products. We hear much of standardizing prices and products, but there is only one justification for standardization, and that is to set a new level. When you standardize prices and products, in order to retain that standard, you arrest progress in the art, and such progress is the most important element in efficiency in industry.

Now, what these experts have said in regard to the course of industry in America during the last twelve years is illustrated by the steel rail controversy of which you have read much during the last year. Of course, the demand upon a steel rail today is much greater than it was thirteen years ago. The weight of trains is greater, as well as the speed. But you have this remarkable fact that, despite all of the possibilities that inhere in American steel rail manufacture, the steel rail industry, for some reason, did not keep pace with the demand for more efficient rails; and you have that continuing condition during the period when, as the reports of the Corporation Commissioner and of the Stanley Committee show, the steel trust was making steel rails at a cost which left the trust an operating profit of nearly $13 a ton out of the $28 paid for the rail. Now, making full allowance for the increase in the demand upon the steel rail, the deficiency in these rails shows what comes from that standardizing of processes, which it is said is the avenue by which a monopoly may conceivably reduce costs.

These facts, to which I have called attention, have made our people appreciate better than they did before, the great economic truth which was embodied in the Sherman Law—have made them appreciate the value of competition. But discussion has done far more than that. While it has made us understand better the value of competition, it has also made us understand defects in the Sherman Law.

These defects are in its application and in the machinery for its enforcement. The law has grave defects. It has, among other things, the defect of uncertainty of application. Since the Supreme Court has declared that only those combinations are illegal which are unreasonable, there is the lack of certainty as to what is or is not unreasonable. Here is a wide field for legal improvement for which legal invention is demanded. These twenty-two years under the Sherman Law have supplied us with experiences which can be utilized to good purpose. We have learned to lay down the rules deducible from that experience, in order to determine, in large measure, what is unreasonable. A practice is unreasonable which tends to destroy competition. And we know now what the main practices are which have been pursued by those trusts to secure the monopoly-control of our industry. They are cut-throat competition, espionage, doing business as fake independents, the making of exclusive contracts, as well as many other methods and practices of unfair trade which have been pursued not for the purpose of conducting a business in competition with others, but for the purpose of killing competitors.

Again, we have found grave defects in our legal machinery. The results of the alleged disintegration of the tobacco trust and of the Standard Oil trust have made these defects obvious; and the LaFollette-Stanley bills proposed to remedy these defects through the exercise of legal invention, just as they undertake also to remove uncertainty in the application of the Sherman Law. Take this instance: When the Court undertook to divide the tobacco trust with a view to restoring competition, the principal properties were distributed among three corporations, which, it was supposed, would compete diligently with one another; and yet the Court seemed to consider itself powerless to prevent such a disposition of the properties as left each of these three corporations to be owned by the same persons in the same proportion! That result was treated as if it were the necessary result of existing rules of law. If such was law, obviously the law ought to be changed. It ought to be not only a possible but a necessary provision in disintegrating trusts, that the several fragments into which the trust is ordered to be divided, should, for a limited period at least, be owned by different groups of stockholders instead of being owned by the same persons.

The La Follette-Stanley bills, which I have not time now to discuss in detail, contain many provisions which have for their purpose to do for trust legislation what has been done by mechanical inventors for thousands of machines in our factories—to make perfect the machine that a good principle may work.

But besides making the Sherman Law certain, and providing legal machinery, we need administrative machinery. We need in industry, as in our cities, in addition to the prosecuting attorney, the inspector and the police. You hear much said of correcting most abuses by publicity. We need publicity; but as a pre-requisite to publicity, we need knowledge. We must know, and know contemporaneously, what business—what big business—is doing. When we know that through an authoritative source, we shall have gone very far toward the prevention of the evils which attend the conduct of business.

We need also ample power in a government board to aid the small man as against his mighty opponent. Some of the finest patriotism which this country has known in the last ten years has been exhibited by small men who, at the risk of destruction, have been willing to aid the government in its effort to secure enforcement of the Sherman Law. We need a board which will protect these men, and in protecting their interests it will protect the interest of the whole community. For that we need an administrative board or commission of some kind.

But we need more than that. I said we need knowledge; I should say over and over again, we need knowledge—comprehensive, accurate, complete knowledge of what is being done in business. And the striking fact today is the absence of such knowledge. We know reasonably well the practices of great and conspicuous trusts which have secured monopoly. We do not know of the agreements and relations of the businesses which are competitive, of those trade agreements, those mutual relations between competitive businesses. In other words, we know the facts in regard to monopolistic combinations; but we do not know the facts in regard to combinations of competitive concerns. I say we do not know the facts. Of course, we have sporadic, unofficial, and to a large extent, inaccurate knowledge of those combinations. But before we can legislate or act in any way, wisely, upon that great subject—the extent to which competitive businesses may have relations with one another—we need that comprehensive and accurate knowledge, and only a commission can secure such knowledge for us.

Now, the investigations and the discussions of recent years have, as I say, brought before us much that is clear, much that men agree upon, and the field of controversy has thus been narrowed. But there is also much as to which men disagree, and the title of the subject of discussion this evening suggests the great and fundamental difference of opinion.

"Shall we regulate competition, or shall we regulate monopoly?" That means, of course, shall we legalize monopoly, and I take it that the position which is clearly drawn between the views of the new party and of others—and particularly the Democratic Party—is this: The new party claims that private monopoly in industry is in some branches desirable, or at all events is inevitable, and that the effort of the government should be confined to limiting the field of monopoly and preventing the abuses which ordinarily attend monopolies.

The Democratic position, on the other hand, is that private monopoly in industry is never permissible; it is never desirable, and is not inevitable; competition can be reserved, and where it is suppressed, can be restored.

Now there had been some denial that the new party proposes to legalize monopoly. That denial has been based, as I believe, upon the assertion that the new party is endeavoring to preserve competition. So it is. But as I should put it, it is in favor of *competition and monopoly*, and I read, as bearing upon that position, this statement, a very recent one, of its great leader:

"Understand, I am not for monopoly when we can help it. We intend to restore competition. We intend to do away with the conditions that make for monopoly. But there are certain monopolies that we cannot prevent. I understand that the steel trust is not an absolute monopoly, but if it were, what would be the use of splitting up the steel trust into companies controlled by Morgan, Carnegie, and Rockefeller, say? Would it ameliorate conditions at all? Would it make prices lower to the consumer? The wages and the conditions higher to the worker? Don't you suppose that these three fellows would agree on prices and methods unofficially?"

Now, gentlemen, see what that implies. It implies that there are at least some fields of industry in which we are to accept private monopoly, and it indicates something which, to my mind, is far more important even than being divided on the great question whether we shall have monopoly or competition. It implies that there is a power in this country of a few men so great as to be supreme over the law; that the will of the American people as expressed in the Sherman Law—which the American people have steadfastly refused to alter in spite of many efforts—cannot be carried out because of the power of certain individuals; that, whether we like it or not, we must have private monopoly in industry to some extent because of the power held by a few of our fellow-citizens. Realize, gentlemen, what that means. It means that we must state solemnly that the power of the American people to enforce law is not absolute; that there are a few individuals who stand superior to the American people.

This same new party platform pledges its members to work unceasingly to restore an increased respect for law. What will be the respect for law when the people come and declare: "We cannot carry out the will of the American people. We cannot prevent individual men unofficially joining together to do that which the law prohibits?"

This very day, but for the engrossing demands of a political campaign and the interest which centers in it, our thoughts would be upon two great prosecutions which are going on, great criminal proceedings going on in this country, more important in many ways than the questions which we and others are discussing: First, the proceedings at Indianapolis involving the great dynamite plot incident to the Los Angeles and other outrages which occupied our attention a year ago; secondly, the proceedings at Salem, in my own state, where great questions arising out of the Lawrence strike are being investigated. What do these prosecutions signify? They mean that a large part of the American people, desirous of securing the social and industrial progress which this new party in its platform declares to be the end to which political effort should be directed, had concluded that social and industrial justice was not to be obtained by law in America; that there is no longer in America equality before the law; that the rich man has such control over affairs in America that the poor and less able worker cannot secure his rights according to the American Constitution, and they have, therefore, resorted to violence. You yourselves in New York, in the recent proceedings, have seen what lack of respect for the law means; not only our property and our institutions, but life itself, are at stake. And yet, with this great demand staring us in the face, calling upon us to do everything we can to bring the American [people] back to a respect for law, we are told that a few rich and powerful men can defy the law; that their power is so great that there will be private monopoly and we cannot prevent it; and that, therefore, we must content ourselves with seeking to mitigate the evil. Respect for law—supremacy of law—is the great question involved—a question more fundamental, almost, than any other.

But that same interview with the great leader of the new party contains another proposition perhaps equally fundamental in our government. The interview ends with these words:

"Back of all this talk about monopoly and competition is the great question, 'What are you going to do with the women and men?'"

Now, I take it in America that what we are going to do is this: Not to *do* something for the women and the men, but to give the women and the men of America an opportunity to do for themselves. If this opportunity is not what America stands for, then our whole scheme of government is naught. What does democracy involve? What does liberty involve? Not merely political and civil and religious liberty, but industrial liberty also. Is not business today the greatest part of life, not only for men, but also to a large extent in the life of women? There are seven million women who have invaded industry. What America needs is not that we do for these, our fellow citizens, but that we keep open the path of opportunity to enable them to do for themselves. When these Americans come to do for themselves, they find this situation: The trust is not merely a capitalistic control of men. It is the worst form of capitalistic control. It is absentee capitalistic control. One hundred and fifty thousand persons are said to interested as stockholders in the steel trust. What have these one hundred and fifty thousand persons to do with controlling the steel trust? The steel trust is a conspicuous instance of ownership separated from responsibility. The steel trust presents a condition similar to that which led to the demoralization of Ireland—the condition of absentee landlordism. The managers may be good men, and true, but the permanent separation of ownership from control must prove fatal to the public interest. The responsibility of ownership is lacking. If there had been responsibility of ownership in the steel trust, it would have been impossible that, with the huge profits of the corporation, which the Commissioner of Corporations found to be $650,000,000 in ten years, in excess of a fair return upon the capital originally invested in that concern, men would have been compelled to work twelve hours a day, seven days in a week, and at such low wages that even if they worked three hundred sixty five days in a year, seven days in a week, their year's earnings would have been less than was necessary; as the minimum amount necessary, in the city of Pittsburgh for the support of a man, his wife, and three children with the minimum of decency. Alas!

7

# An Economic Exhortation to Organized Labor

*This speech on what Brandeis felt unions should do to secure their future was given to the Boston Central Labor Union on February 5, 1905. It was published in the March 15, 1905, issue of* Civic Federation Review.

Trade unionism has made great advances within the last three years. The growth in membership has been large, but the change in the attitude toward unions both on the part of the employer and of the community marks even greater progress. To this result, the anthracite coal strike, so wisely led by John Mitchell, has largely contributed. That struggle compelled public attention to the trade union problem in a degree unprecedented in this country.

The arbitrary attitude of the presidents of the coal and railroad companies was an object lesson which made clear to many employers the unreasonableness of the position that an employer "must be free to run his own business in his own way."

From this warning example, many employers learned also that one may deal with employees otherwise than directly or individually, and that the representatives of unions may be recognized without impairment of usual business honor. Since then, it has become far more common for enlightened employers, whether their shops be union or open, to discuss labor problems with the representatives of the unions as freely as they would discuss other problems with other business connections.

The people at large who had no special interest in contests between employers and employees learned also through the coal strike much about unions. Sympathy was generally with the men as against the coal trust. Even among employers there were many who realized that their interests lay with the workingmen as against the great aggregations of capital.

Sympathetic attention being drawn to the unions, many people realized that the aim of the unions was in the main commendable, even if particular measures of unions or acts of individual unionists deserved condemnation—for who could deny that the work of the unions in seeking to improve the conditions and to shorten the hours of labor, to raise wages—to protect children and women—made for good citizenship and the general welfare of the community? The attitude of the American Federation of Labor in opposing socialism is also gaining for the unions support from the most conservative classes.

A substantial advance has thus been made by the unions in the estimation of working men, of employers, and of the public.

The achievements of the unions in improving the lot of the laborer are not to be measured solely by conditions in the union shop or even in the non-discriminating open shop.

Unions may well point, as their greatest triumphs to certain establishments where no unionist is to be found, but where the conditions of labor are far in advance of the standard ordinarily prevailing. Those are instances where wise, far-seeing employers have acted upon the spirit or hint of union demands.

These steps in advance have been taken often for the purpose of preventing trade unionism from finding a lodgment, often unconsciously as a result merely of the enlightenment that comes with the necessary thinking that trade-union agitation compels.

So, the unions have already achieved much, both directly and indirectly, in shortening the hours and in improving the conditions under which labor is performed, and in raising wages.

How far can this increase in wages be carried, and how shall it be accomplished?

*First*—The unions should strive to secure for the workingmen all the earnings of a business except that part which is required to get for it the necessary capital and managing ability.

Into most businesses three elements enter: 1, the capital; 2, the ordinary labor; and 3, the special labor, usually called the "management."

The owners of capital are comparatively few in number; the possessors of the special ability to manage business still less in number; men competent to perform the ordinary labor very numerous.

Obviously in our country we should strive to conduct our industries as we do our government; that is, to secure the greatest good for the greatest number. The employees being the greatest number, [they] should get of the fruits of the business as much as possible. This is clear. The question is merely, what are the limits now possible, and how can those limits be extended?

It is absolutely essential upon any scheme of division of the fruits of industry among employer, capitalist and employee that the business should be profitable. By "profitable" I mean not merely that the business shall not be run at a loss, but that the business shall be run under such conditions that the owner of the capital on the one hand is willing to risk his capital in the business, and the possessor of that special ability which is required to organize and conduct a successful business will be led to use his greatest efforts in that direction.

Unless the profits of businesses are such as to tempt capitalists to risk their money, the money will seek, not participation in business, which necessarily involves great risks, but will be put into classes of investment where there is supposed to be no risk whatever.

Unless men of exceptional business ability have the promise or possibility of large rewards they will not be led to develop or use those special talents or capacities which we find in the leaders of great businesses—the men who have made or managed them.

What the exact amount of profit is which is necessary to make men risk their money in business, and how great the rewards must be in order to develop the leaders of industry are, of course, matters which cannot be decided by any general rule.

*Second*—The employees should strive to make the earnings of any business as large as possible.

There can be no greater mistake for the workingman than to restrict the output of the individual.

You must make the total earnings of the business in which you are engaged the largest possible. By earnings in this connection I mean the aggregate fund available for paying workingmen, capitalists and managers. Make that aggregate large and there will be plenty for all among whom it is to be divided.

The most potent factor in securing large profits is the avoidance of waste, and the greatest source of waste in the industrial world is unused, undeveloped or misdirected human effort. To the correction of that evil, trade unions should direct their attention.

Let everyone engaged in the business work with the greatest possible efficiency and diligence consistent with maintaining himself in good condition to work thereafter and leaving himself the leisure necessary to the performance of his duties to his family, to his state and for his own development and pleasure.

The hours of labor should be reasonably short; but during working hours each individual should work hard and earnestly, and under conditions leading to the greatest possible efficiency.

Any restriction upon the output of the individual reduces the fund of profits available for distribution, besides demoralizing the man who is so restricted.

It follows also that differences in efficiency between different individuals must be recognized and rewarded; and that those who can work faster and better than others must not be retarded by the less efficient. The industrial superiority of America is largely due to the absence of restriction upon individual effort; to the encouragement of the individual by giving him the fruits of his labors.

Your federation opposes socialism, but to ignore the difference between individuals would lend strength to socialism and communism.

A limitation of the production of the individual is pure waste. The business is merely rendered less profitable, and the man whose production is restricted is injured also.

Nor does the restriction of the output of the individual make more work for others. The amount of work to be done is, in a country like ours, in no sense fixed; for the amount of goods or service men buy is not fixed. The amount bought is as a rule limited only by the ability to buy.

If you waste human effort, you make the product cost more. If you raise prices without increasing income, you have simply limited the amount that will be bought. You have not made work for more people. You have merely given people less for their money.

Another great factor of waste in most businesses is the cost of inspectors, foremen and assistant foremen—men whose services are in large part required only because so many employees work, not as hard or as well as is possible but only hard enough or well enough to pass the inspector or foreman.

Every man should look out for himself, should do the work without inspector or foreman watching him like a policeman. The dishonor and the expense of unnecessary inspectors and foremen should be avoided.

Trade unions have already done much for the manhood of the workingman. They should teach him that it is a disgrace to manhood to require watching.

*Third*—The unions should demand for the workingman steady work.

In order that the pay of the individual may be large, it is necessary not merely that the business as a whole be profitable, but also that the individual be given full opportunity to work for his share of the profit.

Most controversies between employers and employees have arisen upon claims for what is called higher wages; that is, for a higher rate per day or per piece. But the rate per day or per piece is only one of the factors which go to make up wages.

The important question is not how much a man is paid per day nor how much per piece, but how much can he earn in a year. He may have high wages and an opportunity of working only half the year.

For instance, it appeared to the anthracite coal strike inquiry that the men worked only about 181 days in the year. Speaking roughly, men should work 300 days in the year.

Lack of earnings is only a small part of the evil which results from irregularity of employment. It is the uncertainty as to a job which produces a large part of the care of a workingman's life, and the days of enforced idleness which [lead] to most of the bad habits.

Every man should have the opportunity of working every day in the year excepting Sundays and holidays and such time as he properly wishes for a vacation. In some trades this is impossible, but in many trades where the irregularity of work is accepted as a necessity, it would be found that if the effort were duly made the amount of slack time could be greatly reduced.

Where men are engaged in trades which on account of the physical conditions can be followed only during a part of the year, there ought to be found for them work at some other trade for the remainder of the year.

No industrial condition can be satisfactory which does not tend to remove the thing called "day labor," which does not seek to make the work of the workingman as steady as that of the clerk or salesman.

No adequate effort to provide against irregularity of work has been made. If the unions once formulate demands for steady work and co-operate with employers to secure it, an immense improvement on these lines will undoubtedly result.

Steadiness of work is nearly as important to the employer as to the employee. For instance, the great aim of the manufacturer must be to run his factory full all the time. Many factories can earn their profit only if they do. If the factory runs all of the time, and the employees work all of the time, it is obvious that the owner can be satisfied with a much smaller rate of profit and the men can be satisfied with a smaller rate per day or per piece than they would have to get if the factory and the employees were idle part of the time.

The manufacturer and the men will get less per piece, but more in the aggregate, and if you can keep the price low the demand for the article, whatever it may be, will be increased.

That is, if you can get your goods cheaper and yet have the men who make them earn in the aggregate as much as when the price of the goods was higher, you are increasing the amount of work, not diminishing it. In other words, it is by increasing the output per man, not by restricting it, that you give work to more men.

And therefore, every bit of efficiency that you can add to the ability of an individual, and every bit of waste that you can avoid and thus enable the goods to be turned out cheaper, will increase the number of consumers, and increase the number of men employed, and increase your own means of comfort and improvement.

*Fourth*—The unions should adapt their demands to the conditions of a particular business.

In order to determine how large a part of these earnings of any business you can properly demand, it is essential that your representatives should understand the conditions of the business.

It is not sufficient that you should make a demand and have that demand assented to or refused. Your representatives must be able to understand the needs and the possibilities of the business you are engaged in.

John Mitchell was successful in the anthracite strike because he understood the conditions of the businesses of the employers and they did not understand the workingman's side of the question.

Your representatives must understand not merely the general line of the business, but the possibilities and the necessities of the particular business in which your demands are to be applied. Concerns engaged in the same line of business in one part of the country and in another, or even in the same community, have varying possibilities and necessities, and your demands must be tempered by those possibilities and necessities.

The possibilities of employers' businesses vary like the employees' capacities. If you attempt to apply rigidly uniform rule to all, you may kill the goose that lays the egg; and except in extreme cases, the goose must be kept alive whether the egg be golden or not.

Don't assume that the interests of employer and employee are necessarily hostile—that what is good for one is necessarily bad for the other. The opposite is more apt to be the case. While they have different interests, they are likely to prosper or to suffer together. Like in the case of dealer and customer, co-operation and a mutual regard for the others' rights are essential to continued success.

This is the lesson unions should teach.

8

# The Desirable Industrial Peace

*In this speech given to the Industrial Department of the National Civic Federation on April 25, 1905, Brandeis outlines his belief that not only are unions necessary for the welfare of the workingman, but they are also essential for liberty. It was published in the May 15, 1905, issue of* Civic Federation Review.

Gentlemen: We do want industrial "peace with liberty," but in this country, at least, material well-being is an essential condition of liberty. In most trades some form of union of employees is required for the attainment or preservation of this liberty. The single workman, standing alone, is in the power—at the mercy, of his employer. The union, while it works for liberty in curbing the power of the employer, necessarily restricts in some measure the freedom of its members. This is an inevitable incident of organization. To secure the benefits of society, including political and civil liberty, we surrender to society a large part of the rights and privileges man would be free to exercise in a state of nature. The trade union exacts from its members no more.

It is not true that the "success of a labor union" necessarily means a "perfect monopoly." The union, in order to attain or preserve for its members industrial liberty, must be strong and stable. It need not include every member of the trade. Indeed, it is desirable for both the employer and the union that it should not. Absolute power leads to excesses and to weakness. Neither our character nor our intelligence can long bear the strain of unrestricted power. The union attains success when it reaches the ideal condition, and the ideal condition for a union is to be strong and stable, and yet to have in the trade outside its own ranks an appreciable number of men who are non-unionists. In any free community the diversity of character, of beliefs, of taste—indeed mere selfishness—will insure such a supply, if the enjoyment of this privilege of individualism is protected by law. Such a nucleus of unorganized labor will check oppression by the union as the union checks oppression by the employer.

The cause of industrial liberty will ordinarily be best subserved by an open shop in which a strong union has a predominating influence. But it is not true that the closed shop—that is, the shop open to all willing to become union men, and to such only—will never give us peace with liberty. The union shop is not necessarily prejudicial to industrial liberty; its adoption may, at times, be indispensable to the attainment or preservation of liberty. The conditions in a trade may be such that the union must, temporarily, endeavor to enforce the union shop by every legal means in its power.

Such a condition arises, for instance, where the employer, while pretending to run an open shop, is actually and insidiously discriminating against union men. It may arise even if the employer's attack be an open one. In such cases, adoption of the union shop becomes a proper war measure. It may possibly, even in the absence of direct attack by the employer, be at times an instrument which it is desirable to use temporarily in order to secure for the union the strength necessary to enable it to exert a predominating influence in the trade. The analogy to the tariff protection of infant industries suggests itself.

Again, if the conditions of a trade are such that non-union labor can find a fair field for employment, the existence within that trade of shops which are open only to union men may be most conducive to the general welfare. The union then works out its regulations and demands under the spur of the competition of non-union shops. The non-union employer works out his relations to labor under the spur of unionism, the knowledge that only very enlightened self-interest can prevent the union from finding lodgment in his establishment, or the loss of his best employees attracted elsewhere by conditions secured in union shops.

If then, the union shop may be at times an effective measure for securing the existence or the efficiency of the union, which is in itself essential to the industrial liberty of the employees, its introduction should not be condemned absolutely and without qualification, unless it be that the union shop is necessarily illegal as infringing some fundamental inalienable right of the employer or of non-union workmen. There are indeed a few cases in some of our inferior courts which seem to declare that agreements with employers to establish the union shops are illegal as interfering with the employer's "right of contract," as unjustly discriminating in favor of one class, and thereby interfering with the workman's "right to work," and as tending to create a monopoly. None of these positions seem tenable.

It does not interfere with the employer's right of contract to induce him to enter into a certain contract. Every contract which any person enters into interferes in some way with his future freedom of contract or other action. That is the very purpose of entering into a contract. The "right of contract" is the right to restrict one's freedom of action. This sacred right of contract is limited only by the requirements of public policy as expressed either in rules of the common law or of statutory prohibition. The privilege for which employers have most strenuously contended in the past is the right to employ, that is to contract with, whom they please—union or non-union men. The employer exercises this privilege when he elects from day to day, to employ union men. No sufficient reason suggests itself why he should not be permitted to agree in advance for a limited time, or until further notice, that he will employ only union men.

It is not an unjust discrimination against certain workmen, or an interference with, their right to work, for a private employer to employ only persons of a certain class. Nor does an agreement to make his selection on such lines, however capricious or unreasonable, interfere with any one's rights. A discrimination between two classes of workmen cannot be unjust unless there is a right not to be discriminated against, in other words, a right to equality of treatment. So far as relates to private employment, there is no such right. The right to work for a private employer is merely the right to be allowed to work if one can find a willing employer.

An agreement to employ union men only undoubtedly tends in some degree to a monopoly, but the tendency ordinarily would be very slight and remote. It certainly is not the law that every contract which tends however slightly towards the creation of a monopoly is unlawful. If it were, no large manufacturer could contract to increase his plant, for such a course tends inevitably towards securing a larger share of the market, thereby driving out competition and to that extent tending towards a monopoly.

In the case of strikes, employers usually assert with much vehemence that in the absence of intimidation, violence, or coercion, the places left vacant by union strikers could be readily filled by non-union men. It is conceivable that the union control in one or all branches of trade might become so great or be exercised in such a manner as to present the evils attendant upon monopoly and call for intervention by law. But if that time should come, there would be no occasion for agreements to employ exclusively union men.

Experience—the natural law in the industrial world—will alone teach us the best course to be pursued, and that course, when laid out, will doubtless follow eventually the lines of liberty.

In the first place, liberty on the part of the employer to agree with the union for a closed shop whenever the inducements offered are sufficient to lead him to voluntarily renounce for a time his absolute freedom to choose such workmen as he pleases. Then, a recognition by the unions that their interests will be best subserved by omitting all attempts to restrict the choice of the employees and devoting their efforts to increasing the attractions of unionism for the workmen, and to removing the incidents of unionism most objectionable to the employer. The wisest labor leaders have already taken this position, and have among other things, declared the policy that the union label must be regarded as a valuable privilege to be acquired through assent to the closed shop, but that where such assent and hence the union label are withheld, the union workman may still work side by side with his non-union brother.

The union label means today goods made in a union shop. It may come to mean goods made under union conditions, whether produced in a closed or an open shop. Whichever its meaning in a given case, the [label] is the most appropriate means of conveying information to which every citizen in a free country who is interested is entitled. It is an instrument of persuasion, not essentially differing from the manufacturer's trademark, under which he seeks to induce customers to buy only a certain brand—"None genuine without our label." The Consumers' League adopts the same method of informing the public what articles are made under conditions it regards as fair and wholesome, and urging special favor for such goods by the consumer. To prohibit the use of such means of conveying information would appear to be an appreciable abridgement of the right of free speech. To prohibit American citizens from acting upon such information would be a serious infraction of their liberty.

We want industrial peace with honor—not the honor of the combatant, but that honor which "is the finest sense of justice that the human mind can frame" and which in a democracy must include something of fraternity as well as liberty.

In such a peace—with liberty, justice and fraternity—and hence with honor, the public is profoundly interested, because it involves the whole future, the success or the failure, of democracy. And the public which is so interested is not "three quarters of the American people" but the whole.

9

# Address of Mr. Brandeis

*This is a transcription of a speech Brandeis gave to the Annual Banquet of National Cloak and Suit Buyers Association on February 14, 1911, about the end of the New York City garment workers strike, which Brandeis helped moderate. It was published in the February 15, 1911, issue of* American Cloak and Suit Review.

Mr. Chairman and gentlemen: I thank you most heartily for this reception, which I am sure is not meant for me alone, but for those gentlemen without whose aid it would have been impossible for me to be of any assistance to those of you here engaged in the cloak trade; in that struggle, those gentlemen, who, like myself, were outside of the trade. But what we have accomplished has been due in a far greater measure to the extraordinary character of the men who represented the manufacturers at that time, men in the cloak trade in this country. I have been engaged in one way or another in an attempt to arbitrate matters and have been occasionally successful in settling disputes. I am sure there has been no occasion, and the men engaged in that dispute have met the problem with greater intelligence, with a finer spirit and with greater courage than those who acted last summer. And it was for that reason, because of what they did and the spirit which those men showed, that I was particularly anxious to be with you tonight. And when there came to me, as the chairman has suggested, the idea that we were coming to a gathering that was not to be a shop conference but to be a coming together, I was appealed to mightily, because I recognized in that word of "get-together" the keynote of what seems to me the situation, not only in business but in the social world today. It marks the tendency of today; the underlying spirit is opposing what was the spirit of a quarter of a century or indeed of a decade or less, ago. Then the cry was every man for himself, and as an incident of it, the devil take the hind-most. We have gotten far beyond that. Experience has taught us the absolute untruth of that as a social and a business doctrine. There is no such thing as every man for himself; the very idea of business belies it. Business means commerce, it means relations, and so closely are our relations bound together that a man who stands by himself must, in spite of an apparent temporary success, in the long run fail in the things that are most worthwhile in business. As in business, so it is in the social world, that we have repudiated the idea that every man is for himself because we have recognized that in this country, we are educated to the proposition that not only are men to be free but they are to have equal opportunity. The constitution of America will not permit that an individual or that large masses of our people shall advance from sacrifices of our brothers. I take it, therefore, gentlemen, that when we meet under the auspices to get together, that means fellowship; it means brotherhood in business, and in all the important relations of life.

Now, in the contest which has been referred to and adjusted last summer, we have what appears to be the most striking demonstration of the truth of that proposition. The strike itself—what caused it? There were abuses, grave abuses, in many of the factories. Many were unsanitary. In many of them there were excessive hours of labor, in many of them wages were inadequate, in many of them men were treated unfairly, even in those relations of the contracts which they had entered into. Now, while that was true of many, while it gave the opportunity and gave the spirit to the men which brought on that strike, there were other manufacturers who were absolutely innocent of each and every one of the causes which led to the outbreak. What good did it do to them? It rained upon the just and unjust alike. They found no matter how carefully they had looked after their individual relations with the men in their shops, no matter how just they had attempted to be, and not only just but generous to the individuals, it helped them not. Why? Because in this society in which we live, men cannot stand alone, they will not be judged wholly by their own action. Why? Because they are responsible not only for their own action but to that extent to which they may be able to govern the action of those with whom they are associated, and that word, that phrase, with whom they are associated is used in a very large and very broad sense. We are necessarily doing what we will. We shall be held up to the responsibility of being our brother's keeper, and our brothers will be held up to the responsibility of being our keeper, that is what "get-together" means. And at no time in society as it exists today can we escape from that position. This relation was recognized by the manufacturers themselves. They saw, every man there among them saw, that it was necessary to band the manufacturers together. What followed from that? When they came to deal with these abuses, when they came to consider one after another the grievances which were presented at our conferences, every man there, whatever he may have thought of unionism, however much he may have abused unionism in the abstract, when it came to dealing with the propositions before them, they recognized that a strong union of the workingmen was absolutely essential to carry out the wishes of the manufacturer. That was in theory. That wasn't on the ground of ordinary moral grounds, any question of ethics merely as they present themselves in men's desires and aspirations as distinguished from the necessities of the occasion. It was a perfectly practical business problem.

How are you going to do away with the abuses which exist in shops that were bringing discredit upon the better class of manufacturers? It could be done only by winning to the manufacturer, by joining and cooperating with the manufacturer of a body of men who to the extent of their ability through organization would endeavor to enforce as best they might the rules which everybody recognized to be necessary to the conduct of business on the plane in which the committee of the manufacturers fully recognized that this business should he conducted. It wasn't necessities of men; it wasn't necessities put upon you by any force of the union. It was the necessities of the situation. You have to deal with human beings. They are the persons with whom you must deal in working out your problems and a strong union was just as essential to the solution of the problems that confronted the trade as a strong employers' association. What were the employers working for and what were the unions working for? Were not they working every one of them, for the things which every man here must stand for, if he is a man, if he is an American, if he appreciates what America offers him and must offer every other man?

I was talking this evening to one of the members of the executive committee and then overheard his discussion with another gentleman, not a member of the committee, and he said was there one thing, was there one grievance which we met that we ought not to have met? But were there? Is it reasonable that men should live and work, particularly that they should work because they have come into direct relations with the trade they should work under sanitary conditions? Is there an American citizen who would have men work under any other than sanitary conditions? If so, he is unworthy of the opportunity which America affords.

We all desire good citizenship. We all quarrel with the American who does not exercise the duties of American citizenship to keep our politics and our government what it should be. I ask you is there any man here who can perform his duties as a citizen who is subjected, in order to get his living, working excessive hours, twelve and fourteen, or even ten hours a day, with any regularity?

Everybody who undertakes to perform his duties as an American citizen knows that it is an absolute bar to his doing so unless he can, after he has left his business, have something of strength and freshness and vitality in him, in order that he may give his time to the state which is protecting him.

There you have one of the things that the men were asking for, and what they were asking for more than anything else. It was a demand which, among a body of merchants, was to be recognized at once as being a supreme necessity of fairness, that is, that men should have an opportunity of presenting properly their side of the bargain. That one body of men, no matter how honest they are and how just that they may appear should have passed to them others who were looking out for the side of those other persons and that is what the labor union undertakes to do. Now, I say, therefore, that every demand that was made, although it may have been presented as a demand of the working people, was a demand which every man here should welcome and must, as an American citizen, welcome just as much as the member of the union. They demand that they have an opportunity of becoming worthy American citizens, and if every man needed that opportunity, it was the men, a large part of those who come here, who in the past had been denied all those privileges, which we citizens of a free and enlightened country have fortunately had all the most of our lives.

So, I say when we come to consider, when we come to real get-together, we have got to think of the men who are not here, of the men who are making life possible. Dr. Hall has said grace for those who are here, but, in this problem of get-together, we find a problem which extends from far beyond the mere manufacturer and his man. All the trade is interested. I found last summer, when I was here attempting to accomplish some results in connection with the strike, friends and clients came to me, jobbers, mill owners, they were interested, very deeply interested, although apparently they had nothing to do with this problem, just as the retailers were interested in the solution of that problem, and just as we found after awhile there was a very potent influence, the tradesmen of the east side were deeply interested in that problem. There you have the independence of all—the whole society is in that get-together, which your toastmaster has referred to, and so it should be, and the distinction of those who are interested directly and those who have direct responsibilities I take it is confined only to this. Every trade has to my mind a foot stand in the community according to the men who are in it. Every trade can be made as honorable as the most distinguished profession. It is up to the men in the trade to make it a profession. Whatever advantage the older professions may have had is an advantage which seems to me to be only temporary, because as I conceive the world as it develops, the business world, it is all to be professional lines.

There has been a great deal said about the commercialism of the profession. A great deal has been rightly said, but I think that the future that is before us is very much brighter than the present or the past. Men are going to find that business, every branch of business, is going to open opportunities of development where the man who succeeds is not the man who has amassed wealth and retired either to banking or to indolence, but it is the man who so advances the business, who so organized and helps organize and develop the business, that he will find the greatest satisfaction and the greatest honor is having lent his aid in the development of that business in which he has spent his most active years.

That has been my belief for a long time and I have had the great fortune in seeing among some of my friends and clients that hope realized and realized in a very high degree, one of the noblest and ablest men whom I have ever known, William H. McElwain, a shoe manufacturer, who was my client for nearly all the years that he was in business came to me. He was an idealist and he pictured to me what his life was going to be.

He was attracted by the profession. He was not a college man, he left school at 14 or 15 and went into one of the shoe factories in Boston. He pointed out to me how he was becoming successful. He was then very young, only 28 or 29 years old; how in a few years he would have prospered and then going to retire from business and was going to study law, and he was going to devote himself to the more public side of the profession.

I turned to him and I said, "No, don't do that, you are a man that we need in the shoe business. Your ideals and your ability have their place there." And as he thought the matter over, he came to the conclusion that was the fact that the shoe business, that very thing in which he had been engaged since he was a boy, that was the place where he could do the great work for society and attain the most honorable distinction, and when he died, as he unfortunately did at the age of 41, he had made the shoe business a science and he had attained a position of operating the greatest factory that that business had ever had.

Now what he did for that business has been carried forward by his associates. What he did for that business can be attained, in my opinion, and will be attained for every business. Men will regard their business as the finest thing on earth. They will regard their business as the one worthy subject for their comfort. There they will seek honor and distinction and satisfaction in removing every blemish upon it, in removing every abuse and every injustice that exists in connection with it.

The clothing business will be a science and a profession because the problems of today, the unsolved problems of today, will engage the attention of the men in them. They will recognize abuse not as something to be apparent, not as something to be avoided by the individual, but as something to be removed, as a problem to be solved, and the best means will be given as the best hours will be given to the solution of that problem.

Now, what made matters so interesting, so particularly interesting to me as I had to grapple with your problems for a short time last summer, was to see the possibilities that there were in that situation and to see the spirit with which the members of the executive committee of the manufacturers grappled with those problems. How they went on and developed under them, and I saw there what I believe is absolutely certain to come, a recognition that whatever is wrong isn't to be borne, but is to be removed, as it can he removed by careful study, by patience and by an uplifting spirit, and above all by that spirit of get-together, that spirit of brotherhood which was suggested by the toastmaster in opening the meeting this evening.

In working out that problem, I believe that you gentlemen here and others will follow the lines which have been entered upon in other professions and other businesses in which I have had occasion, in another connection to speak on, as the science of management; that science of management which starts in with the proposition of carefully investigating every problem as it presents itself with the best mind that can be given to it and solve that problem. There, gentlemen, is the particular subject to which I feel confident you and hundreds of thousands of others will be pressing their minds and their efforts to make your business great, to make your business contribute to the general welfare, to make your business one where you have no occasion to make excuses for any man or body of men in it doing things inimical to the public good. That, gentlemen, is the true get-together, and that is the spirit and manner in which you can make your business as honorable and, in every way, as enjoyable throughout life as the most advanced of professions have already become.

I thank you, gentlemen, for your attention.

# 10

# Menace of Trusts to Labor

*This is an interview with Brandeis conducted by Percy White that ran in the December 31, 1911, issue of the* Boston Post. *Brandeis discusses how unions and laborers have suffered in industries controlled by trusts.*

Dynamiting and murder by men such as the McNamaras[1] result from the sense of despair induced by the despotism of the trusts, according to Louis D. Brandeis, who in an exhaustive analysis of this unfortunate situation, declares that it can be abolished if union labor will but expel all members who advocate violence of any kind.

Mr. Brandeis, the Boston lawyer who abandoned the cause of the trusts in order to plead the cause of the worker, and the man who is considered one of the highest authorities in the country to umpire the unending conflict between these two factions, explains the origin of conditions which make labor leaders resort to dynamite and murder. He portrays the lamentable conditions which make the struggle to the laborer a case either of anarchy or of his own annihilation. He tells just how much the trusts are to be blamed for these conditions. He points out where union labor itself is responsible. He sums up the heavy burden the American workingman has to bear. And he suggests the remedy.

---

1. In September 1910, labor leaders and brothers John J. and James Barnabas McNamara bombed the Los Angeles Times building out of frustration over the newspaper's anti-labor stance. The two brothers had been sentenced to jail a few weeks before this article was printed.

Sitting in his office in that downtown section of Boston where millions of dollars of capital change hands every day, but where his eyes are always open wide for the interests of the workingman, he talked with me of all these matters. My first question was:

*"What did you mean in saying that the employees of some trusts, notably the Steel Trust, 'are nothing more than slaves in the hands of the corporation leaders because of their monopoly'."*

Mr. Brandeis smiled. "That is not exactly what I did say," he replied. "The statement which I made in respect to the relation of the trusts, and particularly of the steel trust, to labor, was this: What has the steel trust done for labor? John Fitch's study of the steel workers of Pittsburgh supplies the answer. 'The formation of the United States Steel Corporation has brought more than 50 per cent of the steel workers of the country under one employer, with the result of uniformity of conditions of labor. In the course of stupendous changes in process and in corporate organization, unionism has been driven out of the mills in the Pittsburgh district. With its elimination has come an increase in hours until the eight hour day has practically disappeared. The majority of employees engaged in processes of making steel work twelve hours. Many work seven days in the week, either without one day of rest or with a free Sunday one week and 24 hours of continuous duty the next. Speeding up methods have augmented production in every department.'

"The increase in the hours and intensity of labor," commented Mr. Brandeis, "has, in spite of the extraordinary earnings of the Steel Corporation, not been attended by corresponding increase in wages. In some departments there have been increases, but less than the increase in the cost of living. In other departments there have been large decreases, in spite of the increase in the cost of living.

"Thus, Fitch states, 'As to wages of the day laborers in 1892, they received 14 cents an hour and homestead. In 1907–1908, their pay was 16 ½ cents per hour in mills of the United States Steel Corporation, an advance of 18 per cent over the hourly pay of 1892. This increase fell short by 4 per cent in keeping pace with the increased cost of necessities as indicated by the Bureau of Labor bulletin.'

"Fitch further states, 'The daily earnings of the men in the crew fell off from 5 to 40 per cent. Had they continued on the eight-hour basis, their loss would have been much greater than it was. As it was, they were not able, in spite of the increase of tonnage they handled, to maintain their old income even by working 12 hours in 1907 as against eight hours in 1892, an increase in the working day of 50 per cent.

"'This degradation of the condition of the laborer was made possible by driving out union labor. The underlying labor policy of the Steel Corporation is the determination to control. In pursuance of which object, the employers exclude the men from any voice in the conditions of their employment. Consistent with this policy, repressive measures have been introduced designed to enable the companies to retain the advantages which they gained for themselves when they eliminated the union.

"'These measures were doubtless intended to preserve industrial efficiency, but they have resulted in the far-reaching censorship that curtails free speech and free activity of the citizen. The effect of these measures is seen in every department of community life wherever in Allegheny county steel is made.'

"The destruction of unionism," Mr. Brandeis explained, "which renders possible such labor condition, has opened broader opportunity in the management of all the powerful trusts. The Standard Oil Trust, the Tobacco Trust, the Shoe Machinery Trust, the Harvester Trust and the Cash Register Trust have all eliminated union labor. The resulting conditions are inconsistent with democracy. They menace our institutions, they prevent the attainment of American ideals.

"At this time, when the American people are stunned by the terrible deeds of trade union officials, and righteous indignation over the unpardonable abuses committed by members of organized labor fills every mind and heart, it is fitting that we should recall the great debt which America owes to the labor unions. To them, in large part, we owe the rise in wages, the shortening of the hours of labor and the bettering of conditions under which employment is performed, and the protection of women and children from excessive or ill-timed work.

"True, the existence of trade union excesses and the disasters which attend them have been enormous—but we believe in democracy despite the excesses of the French Revolution. We must not forget the merits of unionism in our righteous indignation over certain abuses of particular unionism.

"Industrial liberty should attend political liberty. America's lead in the industrial world is due more to the support and ability incident to free people than to its boundless resources. We have led the world industrially not so much because the resources of nature were unbounded, as because the faculties and aspirations of Americans were comparatively unfettered. We must have, for the development of our industry as for the development of our citizens, the highest degree of liberty attainable.

"Industrial democracy should ultimately attend political democracy. Industrial absolutism is undesirable and should be impossible. We must avoid industrial despotism, even though it be benevolent despotism. Our employers can no more afford to be absolute masters of their employees than they can afford to submit to the mastery of their employees. Neither should feel that he stands in the power—at the mercy—of the other. The sense of unrestricted power is just as demoralizing for the employer as it is for the employee.

"Neither our intelligence nor our characters can long stand the strain of unrestricted power. Every business requires competition from without. It requires likewise a certain competition from within, which can exist only where the ownership and management on the one hand and the employees on the other shall each be alert, hopeful, self-respecting and free to work out for themselves the best conceivable condition.

"The powerful trusts have created conditions absolutely inconsistent with America's industrial and social needs. It may be true that as a legal proposition mere size is not a crime, but mere size may become an industrial and social menace because it frequently creates, as against possible competitors and as against employees, conditions of such gross inequality as to imperil the welfare of the employee or of the industry; and in the midst of our indignation over the unpardonable crimes of trade union leaders disclosed at Los Angeles, should not our statesmen and thinkers seek to ascertain the underlying cause of this widespread, deliberate outburst of crimes of violence?

"What was it," Mr. Brandeis continued, "that led men like the McNamaras really to believe that the only recourse they had for improving the condition of the wage-earner was to use dynamite against property and life? Certainly, it was not individual depravity.

"Was it not because they and men like them believed that the wage-earner, acting singly or collectively, is not strong enough to secure substantial justice? Is there not a causal connection between the development of these huge indomitable trusts and these crimes of violence, and are not these indomitable trusts an important contributing cause of such criminal evidences of social unrest?"

*"With regard to what you call 'absolutism of labor' or 'industrial despotism,' do you think that these would be a menace to this country in case labor should eventually gain ascendancy over capital?"*

"I think we should not expect in America that either capital or labor shall be absolute. I think safety demands that each should be reasonably strong so as to protect its rights against the other."

*"You would not, as the socialist would, predict an era in which labor would finally get the upper hand?"*

"I do not predict anything. I am merely pointing out what in the present state of things seems to me a very great menace to our institutions."

*"What have you to say of the methods by which the trusts abolished union labor?"*

"I think, so far as the methods go, it was simply this position: That when you have tremendous inequality in power, that is, you have a concern with concentrated power, like any trust, which is ready for the purpose of carrying out its purposes, whether it be to crush a competitor or to crush a labor union, to expend many millions of dollars thinking they would ultimately reimburse themselves, you have a situation where ordinary labor is absolutely impossible to cope with it.

"The laboring interests have not the cohesion necessary to meet such a situation, and, particularly, they have not the accumulated means which gives them the power of endurance to carry the war to a point where the trusts would have to succumb, and it is that tremendous power of the trust, with its huge resources, which creates the inequality that is dangerous to our social institutions."

*"Do you agree with ex-President Roosevelt that laboring men at times 'show the worst form of class consciousness, that of sinister and brutal class selfishness, in standing by criminals simply because they are of their own class'?"*

"I haven't any doubt but that labor has done that in many instances, all of greater, or less significance. It is the same class consciousness which makes people in other walks of life stand by their fellows and which makes people stand by their brothers, or members of the same club. It is simply an abuse of the admirable trait of loyalty. A party can never be excused fully, and it is generally extremely unwise.

"In respect to labor, it seems to me most clear that it is a condition of the wide success of trade unionism that the unions should undertake to discipline their own members. It is essential that they be their brother's keeper and that they should teach their members that every reprehensible act by a member of the union is treason to the union. It is only by such a course that the union can secure that support from public opinion which the fine purposes of the union entitle it to.

"Whatever criticism is to be passed upon the conduct of the union ought to come, in the first place, from the officers and members of the union itself, and I believe that the recent horrible crimes disclosed at Los Angeles will have a beneficial effect upon the union in this respect. It will make union leaders and union members realize, as they never have before, how important it is for them to keep their membership free from conspicuous wrong-doing."

*"But are the leaders responsible for the conditions which make dynamiting a seeming necessity, or are the members themselves responsible, or is it the defect of [the] institution of labor unionism in general?"*

"Dynamiting is never necessary in any proper sense of that term, and it can never be excused," was the answer. "It must always remain a crime; it deserves to be severely punished. There must be a cause very much deeper to make men resort to such means, not once, but as a broad plan of action. As I stated before, it is the duty of the statesmen and the thinker to endeavor to find out what the real causes are which lead to such crimes in a free country.

"To my mind, they can spring only from a sense of hopelessness and despair of being able to right existing wrongs by any ordinary and legitimate means. Of course, dynamiting can never right wrongs; it is a futile, unintelligent attempt, but the explanation of a resort to such means is, to my mind, clear. It expresses a sense of hopelessness of effort in any legitimate way, and that hopelessness of effort arises from the fact of the great inequality in position and strength of the contending forces—organized capital on the one hand, concentrated, ably directed and with huge resources; laborers on the other hand, but loosely bound together, led by leaders of but meager ability and without resources.

"It is this inequality that produces, by repeated experiences, the sense of hopelessness and despair, and which induces the misguided laborers to resort to criminal means. Our duty is to seek to temper the inequality and to open to the laborer vistas of hope of reasonable success."

*"A few minutes ago, you made reference to the French Revolution. Now you have been speaking of the despairing condition of certain laboring men.*

*In connection with that, you state that dynamiting can never right wrongs. Did the guillotine never right wrongs? In other words, does this McNamara affair not mean, in the long run, a great benefit to the interests of labor?"*

"Any occurrence which calls our attention to a serious evil results in benefit," he answered, "if we are wise enough to utilize the facts called to our attention for the purpose of removing the causes of the evil. If these horrible crimes lead to arousing the attention of the American people sufficiently to induce them to study out the causes which led to these crimes and to exert their efforts to the removal of those causes, all persons in the community, whether they be laborers or others, will be immensely benefited, because, after all, the cause of labor is the cause of the whole community.

"We are in a democracy. We are all brothers; we are bound to be; and although temporarily a few persons may secure such a position as to appear to be independent of the welfare of others, their position is but temporary and their independence is but delusive. We are all bound indissolubly together, and in the end, we must stand or fall together."

*"Ex-President Roosevelt speaks of 'capitalists who have been guilty of brazen corruption and labor leaders who have been guilty of murderous violence.' Is there any panacea for this?"*

"No panacea. Perfection in human interests is not attainable, but it is possible to approach very much nearer than we are today. That approach can be made through the education, not only of the head, but of the heart. We have but to remember the purpose of the founders of our country as declared in the Declaration of Independence. We need only remember that we are a democracy, that our aspirations should be toward the attainment of reasonable equality, not the attainment of actual equality, but by avoiding such inequalities as render real brotherhood on the part of Americans impossible.

"Every American is part of the government and therefore must have a definite effect upon the life of every other American. We are committed, irrevocably, to the proposition that we are all to rise or to fall together."

*"Does the community at large ever gain by the antagonism between labor and capital?"*

"That depends upon what you mean by antagonism between capital and labor. The community undoubtedly gains by the effort of the individuals. If antagonism means merely that capital on the one hand and labor on the other is strenuously looking out for what it deems its own interest, then the community is a gainer by that effort. If antagonism means, however, that labor is endeavoring to crush capital or capital to crush labor, then obviously not only the combatants but the community loses, because the combat results in the extinction of the one or the other."

*"Do you believe with Mr. Roosevelt that the general opinion among laboring men who perform acts of violence is that they are engaged in a justifiable 'war in behalf of their class'?"*

"I have no doubt that very many of the laboring men who, at one time or another, have committed acts of violence in a trade conflict believed they were 'waging war for the benefit of their class,' but the personal equation must not be forgotten.

"Men who engage in a fight are carried away by the spirit of 'war' regardless of its purpose. No doubt in very many instances, labor men have committed violence in the course of a trade 'war' without any thought whatever that they were benefiting labor by so doing; and in many other instances, possibly with the knowledge that they were not benefiting labor but merely because they were fighting and they did what it seemed to them a way of winning, or because they wished for personal reasons to revenge themselves upon some opponent from whose blows they had smarted."

*"What is your opinion as to their culpability as compared with the culpability of the Black Hand?"*

"I think it perfectly clear that no murder is justifiable, and that all murder ought to be punished. In my mind, the important thing is not to dwell upon the particular degree of culpability, but to look deeper and find out what caused the murder and try to remove the cause. It seems to me that all speculation about culpability may well be dropped for the more serious duty of finding out what it was that led the McNamaras to do what they did do, and see whether society as a whole, by giving its attention to that question, cannot prevent a repetition."

*"Will you further express your opinion as to this underlying cause?"*

"I have expressed in the passage quoted from my address before the Senate committee on interstate commerce what I believe, in a large measure, to be the cause. It is an industrial condition under which the working man has lost in many branches of trade his sense of personal liberty, and with it the sense of hope.

"That condition is one which, in some other countries, might exist without producing harmful results. I refer to those countries where the worker does not possess political liberty. But in America, where the individual does possess political liberty, it is essential that industrial liberty should go with it. To deny industrial liberty, and at the same time grant political liberty, creates a condition which must result in social unrest."

*"To sum the whole matter up, what do you consider has been the effect of the McNamara case on the cause of labor in general?"*

"The temporary results of the McNamara case are prejudicial to trade unionism. In course of time, they will produce exactly the opposite results and will lead to a great advance of trade unionism, because the unfortunate occurrences connected with the McNamara case will result, to a certain extent, in the reorganization and purification of the labor union. It will make leaders and members alike understand that the success of unionism means an elimination from the union of violence or other illegal methods, and that it must be the union itself, and not others, who bring about this purification.

"In other words, as I have stated, the union leaders and members will alike learn that the doing of a reprehensible act by a union member is treason to the union, and it will be a sufficient cause for discipline and possible expulsion, and that a unionist has been 'guilty of conduct unbecoming a union member.' When that practice has been established, unionism will have much support in the community and will undoubtedly advance rapidly in influence and power."

*"What, in your opinion, is the most powerful weapon the laboring man can use in an effort to obtain what he considers his rights?"*

"The most powerful weapon that the union can use is to be right," was the quick retort. "That involves, on the one hand, conduct which is not only in accordance with law but in accordance with prevailing ethical standards. On the other hand, it involves a development of the individual to his highest efficiency. When unionism means not only good behavior but good workmanship and the assurance of proper effort by the working man to perform his duty, the community will give general support to the effort of the working man to increase his wages, to shorten the hours of labor and improve the conditions under which work is done."

*"What, in a word, should be the natural rights and perquisites of the laboring man?"*

"The purpose of the laboring man must be constant improvement of his material, mental and spiritual condition. America, the great land of opportunity, should offer him a free field for such effort. The fruits of labor should go to labor, and the efforts of labor ought to be legitimately directed to securing for themselves that which is their share of the fruits of industry."

*"What position should he hold in the organized industry of the world?"*

"He ought to hold the highest position that his ability will enable him to fulfill. In other words, positions in industry should come to those who deserve them by their achievement and not as a result of privilege or mere power."

*"Have the trusts robbed the laboring man of these rights and perquisites?"*

"In my opinion," concluded Mr. Brandeis, "the trusts have been the most serious menace to labor by robbing it, in large part, of its liberty. Labor can be potent only in dealing with capital through organization and collective bargaining. It has been the common incident of the organization of powerful trusts, of those which really dominated the field, that they eliminated union labor. No matter how well labor may have been treated by particular trusts, the denial to the individuals of the right of organization and of that development and protection which comes with organization is a denial of the most serious right which labor can possess. It is the foundation of all right. In a country like America, in which our whole government rests upon the freedom of the individual, the evil resulting from such a condition must be apparent."

## 11

# Brandeis on Big Textile Strike at Lawrence and Industrial Democracy

*This is an article written by Brandeis that was published on the front page of the March 17, 1912, issue of the* Boston American. *Brandeis expresses his belief that business owners will flourish when they not only accept unions but also learn to work with them in managing their businesses.*

The Lawrence strike is ended and ended happily. There has been a substantial increase of wages, the increase being largest for those who needed it most.

It is not only Lawrence, but the textile workers of New England who have won by this strike. The increase is also affecting Canadian textile mills. Undoubtedly it will have its influence upon the whole textile industry of America, and probably of the world, in the immediate future.

The conditions disclosed at Lawrence, the existing social injustice and the social dangers of un-American standards of living, will be made manifest to the whole country by the investigators of the United States Bureau of Labor, the correspondents of the press, and eminent magazine writers.

We may be reasonably assured that wages will not hereafter be reduced in the textile industries, and that the changes in wages and conditions will be such as tend to improve the lot of the worker. The social advance so resulting cannot fail to have great influence for the social good.

But the strike has its significance far broader than this. It marks, in a significant way, the beginning of a new era in the relation of employer to employee, of capital to labor.

We have had, and have now in America, an irreconcilable conflict between the political and industrial conditions of the working man. Politically, he is free; industrially, he is dependent. We have in most departments of industrial life, side by side, political democracy and industrial absolutism.

I believe this to be perfectly clear: Our working people will not submit much longer to having their condition of life determined by a few people. They will insist upon having some voice in the determination of the conditions under which they shall work and live. To have such part is an essential of liberty.

From the point of view of labor, either one of two things must happen.

We shall have a great development of unionism, of collective bargaining, or we shall have a socialistic state where the people will work for the State and determine conditions by their vote. Either one of those things must happen.

The question is simply whether we are going to maintain our institutions, along with trade unionism, or make a socialist state inevitable by permitting collective bargaining to be stamped out of existence.

I want to bring out clearly this point. We have reached the time when the worker must have his part in industry through co-operation, through industrial democracy.

It is obvious that present conditions cannot continue. Either our people will lose their political independence, or they will acquire industrial independence. We cannot exist half free and half slave.

I was talking a short time ago with a representative of one of the large successful industries, where the people are extremely well treated and where they employ 6,000 employees.

He has done everything he could to make the conditions of the laborer just and fair, but he won't have any unionism.

He said to me: "We have this property here. We can't run the risk of our property being destroyed by these 6,000 men."

"Well," I said to him, "how can the 6,000 men run the risk of being destroyed by you?" That is the whole thing in a nutshell.

The last twenty years, which have witnessed the growth of the trusts and other great business organizations, have marked likewise the growth of industrial absolutism on the part of the employer as against the employee.

From most of the trusts and large businesses, other than the railroads, trade unionism has been excluded. The condition of the steel worker disclosed by the investigation of the United States Bureau of Labor can be adequately explained only by the fact that the workers were not organized.

The great improvement in the condition of the textile workers, which has resulted from the Lawrence strike, will convince the workers of the whole country of the efficacy of organization.

But it is not only the workers who will thereby be convinced of the value of unionism. Intelligent employers will come to recognize that the interests of capital, as well as the interests of labor, demand a labor condition under which it is possible for the employer to consider from time to time, with an experienced body of men representing labor, the problems of the industry.

It also seems reasonably clear now, with the march of progressive ideas and the pervading interests in social and industrial questions, that the political liberty of the people will become more real and not less, and that the worker will appreciate more than ever before the significance of his part in the industrial system.

Today, in most industries, the responsibility of management and of justice to those engaged rests wholly upon the owners of the capital.

It seems almost too clear for argument that no body of men, that no mill managers or directors, however well-intentioned and however intelligent, are able wisely and justly to decide as between capital and labor what the treatment of labor should be.

It is difficult enough to decide wisely, and justly, if one is disinterested. The interested party cannot be properly entrusted with the decisions which directly affect the lives of thousands of other people.

These people themselves must have a voice in determining the conditions under which they are to work and live, and they cannot have an effective part in determining these questions except through an organization.

Obviously, that organization ought to be a permanent one, one which shall at all times keep itself advised as to the conditions of the industry and as to what may in fairness be claimed by the workers in it. It should also be a continuous body, constantly in touch with the problems and possibilities of the industry, that will gradually assume its proper share in the responsibility for its success.

It should, therefore, be the strong desire of every employer to encourage the formation of strong unions, and to share with those unions the responsibility of management.

In other words, we must secure as between employer and employees real co-operation, not small profit-sharing, which as ordinarily practiced is little more than a contingent addition to wages, but a sharing of responsibilities, which is the real essence of co-partnership.

And it is in such co-operation only that we may look forward to that advance in the condition of the workingman which is longed for, and which the interests of society demands.

There is an obvious limit to the increase of wages possible under present conditions.

If the profits earned in most manufacturing businesses today was applied to paying only a minimum return upon capital, say 4 per cent, and the balance distributed among the employees, the earnings of the employees would be raised so little as to leave their conditions only slightly better than it is today.

In some businesses called profitable, where labor is a large element in the cost of the product, a 10 per cent increase in the labor cost would leave practically no return to capital.

Obviously, a 10 per cent increase in wages would do little for labor, other than relieve immediate necessities. This would leave the great problems of improving the condition of the workingman still unsolved.

What the welfare of the industry and the community demands is a condition of things under which the gains of the industry may be greatly enhanced, so that the condition of labor may become really what it should be in a nation of free men.

To this end, the elimination of waste is essential, and the greatest of all wastes is the failure of men to accomplish all that they might.

Today the efficiency of the employee is greatly limited by his discontent, and by the failure to call upon him to exercise the best that is in him.

The best that is in man will be developed only by putting upon him responsibilities, and by raising a man to his true position of a free worker and differentiating his work most fully from that of the servant or the slave.

It is only through co-operation that such development and efficiency can come, and even then it will come gradually, when the position of the employee is changed to that of partner.

Co-operation between the owners and managers of our great corporations and the thousands of men whom they employ can be rendered possible only through organization of the employees, and their representation through such organization in the businesses of which they form a part.

The main obstacle to the development of trade unionism in America hitherto has been the closed shop, for the American people have been unwilling to run the risk of exchanging the possible tyranny of labor for the existing tyranny of the employer.

The cry for the open shop has, therefore, had the support of public opinion, and trade unionism has made slight, if any, relative advance for many years.

While the closed shop has been thus objectionable, the open shop has not presented an acceptable alternative, because the open shop has involved in most instances the disintegration of the union.

This has been true even where the employer has dealt fairly with the union, and not in secretly discriminating in favor of non-union labor.

Many a workman who rejoices at the benefits obtained for him by the union in an open shop has been unwilling to bear what seemed to him the unnecessary burden of union dues and the restrictions incident to membership in the union, when he got all the advantages whether he belonged to the union or not.

Experience showed, therefore, that the advance in unionism demanded something other than either the closed or the open shop. Some alternative must be found which was consistent with the American demand for freedom and also consistent with the interests of unionism.

It is believed that the solution has been found in the preferential union shop which was introduced in the settlement of the great New York Garment Workers' strike in the summer of 1910, and which has been in successful operation since.

Under that system the employer agrees to give the union men the preference in employment, other things being equal, and adequate provision is made for securing the effective enforcement of this agreement.

In the preferential union shop, all the advantages of collective bargaining are secured, and at the same time there is protection against the abuses which are apt to result from the monopoly and compulsion incident to the closed shop.

It is obvious that the Lawrence settlement is only an adjustment of a single difficulty. Unless something more is done, this great struggle will have resulted simply in letting the future take care of itself, which the future is not apt to do very advantageously to those concerned.

This settlement, to be real valuable socially and industrially, must be followed by some provision which shall avert in the future similar contests. It must be a settlement that shall detect the grievances before they become serious and fester, that shall provide the means for considering from time to time the slight or the serious questions which may arise, and by appropriate consideration prevent or remove abuses, and what is quite as important, prevent all future misunderstandings.

This result can be attained through organization, and can be attained only by that means, and the organization must be of a character to fully represent the workingmen employed and to secure their full support. In other words, the labor of our mills must be organized.

It is obvious too, that the greatest need of business today is stability.

To secure stability through a strike settlement, there must be an assurance of the continuation of the conditions secured by some provision made.

Changes in these conditions will then be wrought through discussion and amicable adjustment, and not through industrial war.

This means, again, that the success of the industry and the welfare of the community can be attained only through a settlement which is followed by some trade agreement, which will bind the employees both of the future as well as the present.

That, of course, necessitates a strong, continuous trade organization.

Under the old conditions, when you had an employer with a few men around him and who he was going to be friends with, and who were going to become employers sometime themselves, you had none of these problems.

Now you have vast numbers dealing with landlordism, where the real owners are away and men managing are in the position of stewards, in the Irish form.

They have to make a good showing, for they have a lot of people depending on them for dividends.

You have a situation which marks a complete evolution of industry, an entirely different situation, and there isn't any way in which the individual worker can get protection except through collective bargaining.

We have in the great industries exactly the situation you have politically in the case of absolutism, an absolute monarch. He may be a benevolent ruler, he may give you an excellent government, but you have no assurance he will not make a terrible mistake.

Absolute monarchy is a fair field, but it has no outlet. That is just the situation in industry, and the more you think of it the more you will see the similarity between the political state and the industrial state.

Everybody has to recognize the abuses of which the unions have at times been guilty. In my own opinion, a very large part of the abuses of unionism have been due to the fact that up to the present time the unionists have been fighting for their lives.

It has been a struggle for existence, and a very bitter struggle. Time and effort have all been given to living. It has been an unequal contest in a large measure, because the men, in loosely organized masses, have been fighting against huge, powerful, unified bodies of employers.

The struggle has been in many cases a desperate struggle—hopeless—where defeat was almost a foregone conclusion.

The men have not only had their time and all their efforts consumed in a large measure in this struggle for existence, but they have been led to resort to methods which can never succeed and which can never be justified.

Instead of fighting organization, the employer ought to encourage it. They ought at the same time to exact from labor the highest standards, and while they approve organization and aid organization, there ought to be an absolute determination not to submit in any instance to the abuse of power. That rule must be enforced, whether the power be in the labor organization or in the capitalistic organization.

I believe when we do reach that point where the labor union doesn't need to spend all its strength in fighting for mere existence, that we shall then get some constructive work. Then all the effort and all the energy and intelligence now in the labor movement will be applied in pushing it forward.

When labor organizations are fostered and the workingmen share in the management of the business, when they have a share in the responsibility for the success of the business in which they work, you will have a great development of efficiency, partly through the good will, partly through the development of responsibility, partly through the added intelligence which comes through the exercise of one's faculties under responsibility.

With such real co-operation, with such a real co-partnership between capital, the managers and labor, will come a great growth in producing capacity. Then the laboring man can, through the increased productivity of business, attain our ideals of an American standard of living without destroying capital, but, on the contrary, giving to capital all to which it may be justly entitled. That can never be done under present conditions, because if you divide all the profits of industry today among the working people, the capitalists will be poorer, but the working people won't be sufficiently richer to make any material difference in the situation.

12

# Laborers as Directors with Boss Possible

*This is an interview with Brandeis that was published in the February 14, 1915, issue of the* Boston Post, *where he again talks about the need for unions' input in managing companies.*

"The question of introducing workers into the boards of directors of big corporations," said Mr. Brandeis to the *Sunday Post* reporter, "is one that must, at present, be treated broadly.

"It cannot be effected merely by introducing a certain number of workingmen into the board of directors. It must come through creating a joint management of the business; that is, giving to its workers a substantial share in the responsibility of management.

"For this purpose, the representatives of the workingmen in the management must be representatives selected not by the employer but by the men themselves. The employees must, through an organization, have the opportunity of knowing the facts concerning the management of the business and of selecting those whom they wish to have represent them in determining the problems which arise from time to time.

"In other words, we must have industrial democracy, and industrial democracy means the participation in the responsibilities of management as well as in the profits of the business.

"A first step, therefore, to participation of labor in the management of the business must be the recognition of the right of labor to organize, because in no other way than through organization can labor participate in management.

"The attainment of industrial democracy is not a matter which can be achieved over night.

"The workingmen must be trained by experience to bear their part in the management of business. That can only come through the gradual yielding to the employees of certain rights which in the past have been exercised only by employers.

"Ordinarily an employer exercises without any outside control the right of employment and of promotion and discharge. There are businesses in which employers, while reserving to the manager the right in the first instance either to discharge men or to deny or grant their promotion, have provided machinery by which the propriety of the exercise of that right may be reviewed.

"This is generally accomplished by means of a board called the board of arbitration to which any employee who feels himself aggrieved, because of discharge or because of a denial of promotion, can present himself, have his case heard, and, if the decision is in his favor, can either be reinstated, with wages for the period since the discharge, or can secure promotion with a compensation for the period in which promotion was denied him.

"In these instances, the members of the board of arbitration are composed in part at least, and sometimes wholly, of men who are in exactly the same position as the employee himself.

"Now, that is a large step toward industrial democracy, but of course only a step.

"Then there are other businesses in which there is a general board chosen by agreement between the employer and the unions. This board undertakes to decide the questions of whether the employer has exercised fairly and reasonably the legal rights which he had, not only of discharge, but of the joint administration of his business so far as it affects employees.

"Under these circumstances, the employer, by agreement with the union, creates a tribunal, a sort of court, also called the board of arbitration, which may pass upon the propriety of the employer's acts. This tribunal is composed wholly or in part of employees.

"Again, in other businesses, you will find arrangements by which the employer has conferred upon associations of employees or some special board, the right to fix the general rules for the conduct of the employees in the business.

"These provisions are similar to those which obtain in many of the women's colleges, where the students form a self-governing body and determine without the interference of the faculty the laws under which they shall live.

"All of these classes of participation by employees in the management of the business are steps toward the recognition of the fact that a business is no longer solely the employer's business. It is the business in which employer and employee are both interested.

"And while these instances as suggested leave the employee, still in many respects subject to the will of the employer, they present a great advance over the old system in which the business was recognized as the employer's business, and the only liberty granted to the employee was either to stay under the rules made for him or to leave.

"This is, of course, a matter which requires preparation on the part both of employer and employee. On the employer's part, it requires rather a conversion. When he is once induced to recognize that safety lies in democracy, rather than autocracy, the long step for him has been taken. Then he is in position to get the advantage of the full benefit of the men's work.

"The great advantage that will then come to business is that the liberation of the employee will add immensely to his efficiency. It will make the employee to a very much larger extent a thinker; it will make him realize that his work is his best field for development, and he will look to that as the employer generally looks to that—as a place for his greatest satisfaction in life.

"The employer constantly says now: 'I am working much harder than any of my employees'—and it is true. But, while he is working harder, he is having the satisfaction which comes with work. The men who are denied participation in the business are denied that satisfaction, and therefore do not in many instances exert themselves to the utmost, although they may be working the full number of hours allotted, and maybe more.

"The problem is to get the most out of themselves, but however much they may wish to get the most out of themselves, they cannot possibly do so unless the conditions are such as to give them satisfaction in what they are doing; and they cannot get satisfaction except through freedom. A large part of the discontent of employees arises from the suppression of their own individuality.

"As a matter of fact, there are few things so interesting in life as work, under proper conditions; and the way that employers generally work establishes the truth of this. They complain because their employees do not work similarly, do not feel the responsibility of the business. Let them give the employees a chance to bear responsibility and the response will come.

"But unrest means ordinarily unused faculties, and there will be labor unrest until the faculties of the laboring man are fully utilized, and they cannot be without a share in the responsibility of the results of the business in which they are engaged.

"At present there is not enough property or enough profits produced to satisfy the reasonable demands of labor, that is the living to an American standard. The only way in which we can hope to attain the American ideals of citizenship for every American is to produce more.

"There ought not to be, therefore, any differences between labor and capital in the effort to produce more; they ought to co-operate fully. The only room for difference that exists is how to share the profits that are made, and unless they make more, labor cannot be satisfied.

"Unless more is made, therefore, there cannot be content on the part of labor, just as there cannot be content on the part of labor unless labor has something to say in the management of the business.

"Without content you cannot have full efficiency. No matter, therefore, how beneficent may be the purpose of the employer in the conduct of his business, he cannot get from the employee full efficiency without content and without the release of his faculties from restraint.

"It is, of course, difficult to effect the transition from an absolutist capitalistic system to a system of industrial democracy, but it must be worked out, and it is being worked out.

"One marked example of what has been and can be done is presented by the co-operative societies, which have attained such extraordinary success in England and Scotland and many parts of Europe, and which are now developing in America.

"The possible forms of co-operation are numerous, but in some form or other, really high efficiency cannot be attained (at least in countries where men are accustomed to democratic ideas) until the workingman feels that he is working, not for somebody else, but for himself and others jointly.

"That is of the essence of industrial democracy. It is the contrast between political democracy and industrial autocracy which is the main cause of the present unrest, and which is a patent cause of the relative inefficiency of men.

"I would urge careful consideration by Americans of the advantages of co-operative enterprises and bid them distinguish clearly between combinations of capital on the one hand and the co-operation of labor and of consumers on the other.

"In a democratic community we naturally long for that condition where labor will hire capital, instead of capital hiring labor. The community should be served either by laborers who hire capital or through those co-operative enterprises, private or public, by which the community undertakes to provide itself with necessaries.

"Of this nature are the retail co-operative stores with all of their adjuncts of wholesale business and manufacturing. Their purpose is to serve the consumer, not primarily to make money.

"Fifty years of growing success of the co-operative movement in England shows what can be accomplished on these lines. It shows also to what extent the ordinary working man may develop under democratic conditions to be manager of 'Big Business.'

"England's 'Big Business' is her Cooperative Wholesale Society. Its annual turnover is now about $150,000,000, an amount exceeded by the sales of only a few American industries: an amount larger than the gross receipts of any American railroad except the Pennsylvania and the New York Central.

"Its business is very diversified. It includes that of wholesale dealer, of manufacturer, of grower, of miner, of banker, of insurer and of carrier. It operates the biggest flour mills and the biggest shoe factory in all Great Britain. It manufactures woolen clothes, all kinds of men's, women's and children's clothing, a dozen kinds of prepared foods and as many household articles. It operates creameries. It carries on every branch of the printing business. It is now buying coal lands. It has a bacon factory in Denmark and a tallow and oil factory in Australia. It grows tea in Ceylon.

"And through all the purchasing done by the society runs this general principle: Go direct to the source of production whether at home or abroad, so as to save commission of middlemen and agents.

"Accordingly, it has buyers and warehouses in the United States, Canada, Australia, Spain, Denmark and Sweden. It owns steamers plying between continental and English ports; it has an important banking department; it insures the property and person of its members. Every one of these departments is conducted in competition with the most efficient concerns in their respective lines in Great Britain.

"The Co-operative Wholesale Society makes its purchases and manufactures its products in order to supply 1399 local distributive co-operative societies scattered over all England, but each local society is at liberty to buy from the wholesale society or not, as it chooses, and they buy only if the Wholesale Co-operative Society sells at market prices. This the co-operative actually does, and it is able besides to return to the local a fair dividend on its purchase.

"Now, how are the directors of this great business chosen? Not by England's leading bankers or other notables supposed to possess unusual wisdom, but democratically, by all the people interested in the operations of the society, and the number of such persons who have directly or indirectly a voice in the selection of the directors of the English Co-operative Wholesale Society is 2,750,000, for the directors of the wholesale society are elected by vote of the delegates of the 1399 retail societies, and the delegates of the retail societies are in turn selected by the members of the local societies, that is, by the consumers, on the principle of one man, one vote, regardless of the amount of capital contributed.

"Note what kind of men these industrial democrats selected to exercise executive control of their vast organization—not all wise bankers or their dummies, but men who have risen from the ranks of co-operation, men who by conspicuous service in the local societies have won the respect and confidence of their fellows.

"The directors are elected for one year only, but a director is rarely unseated. J.T.W. Mitchell was president of the society continuously for 21 years.

"Thirty-two directors are selected in this manner; each gives to the business his whole time and attention, and the aggregate salaries of the 32 is less than that of many a single executive in American corporations, for these directors of England's big business serve each for a salary of about $1500 a year. That shows what industrial democracy can do.

"We in American must come to the cooperative idea. All over this country today co-operative societies are springing up. They rise; naturally many of them fail; but out of the seeds of each failure new ones arise, and with experience comes ultimate success. Every man who is participating, whether as consumer or officer of a co-operative society, is aiding in the development of that industrial democracy, without which America cannot attain her ideals of manhood."

"Have you ever heard of a division of industry into labor, efficiency and capital?" Mr. Brandeis was asked.

"Yes, there have been such suggestions, but it seems to me to be a false division. If there is to be any division, it should be a division between labor and capital. All labor should be made efficient, for there is no labor which is of necessity unskilled labor. If labor is unskilled, it is because the greatest efficiency hasn't been attained.

"Taylor[1] showed the difference between the skilled and the unskilled loading of pig iron into a car.

"It was the simplest hand work to lift a pig of iron from the yard into a car; but by proper skill, that is by scientific management of that simple operation, it was possible to produce nearly four times the result with no greater labor.

"Taylor showed in the same way what has been called the unskilled occupation of shoveling coal, two or three times the amount could be shoveled by the resort to proper methods and the use of proper tools. Shoveling therefore ceased to be an unskilled occupation.

"And so in all lines of business activity rests this opportunity, through care, through planning and through instruction, as well as through invention, to discover methods by which the same result may be achieved with a less waste of effort or of material.

"There ought not to be any division strictly between labor and efficiency, that term I supposed was used to express the management. Management and labor should be one, because the principles of efficient management ought to penetrate every part of the field of labor.

"When that is recognized by all engaged in industry as the aim [to] be attained, productivity will be immensely increased and the remaining demands of all engaged in industry will be satisfied."

---

1. Frederick Winslow Taylor (1856–1915) was a proponent of Scientific Management.

## 13

# Address Before the Cambridge Citizens' Trade Association

*This is a transcript of a speech Brandeis made during a March 25, 1908, debate with various officials from the New Haven Railroad Company. A couple of sentences from the speech were used in Lewis Paper's book* Brandeis, *but this is the first time the speech has been reprinted in its entirety. The typescript for this speech is held in folder NMF 1-l-1a of the Brandeis papers held at the University of Louisville.*

Some corporations are born monopolies, some achieve monopoly, and some have monopoly thrust upon them. Mr. Byrnes would have us believe that the New Haven is of the last class. I ask you to look at the past, to recall the facts within your own knowledge, and to determine whether that is the situation. Mr. Byrnes seems very much afraid of the word "monopoly"—as afraid of the word as I am of the thing!

He says that what he desires is to find some way in which this large stockholder of the Boston & Maine may exert the influence which a large or a majority stockholder should exert. Now, see what that really means. That means for northern New England what has happened in southern New England—not by an accident—that every railroad in Connecticut and Rhode Island and leading into New York—that every trolley line in Connecticut and Rhode Island and the proposed entrance into New York—that every steamship line which in any way connects New England with any point on the Atlantic coast, with the exception of one line in the hands of a receiver—every one of those lines, running from Portland, Maine, down to Savannah, Georgia, has passed into the control of the New Haven—not by accident, not because wicked and designing bankers have come to them and held them up, but because that road, with a deliberate purpose of extinguishing at any cost any competition in transportation, has gone forward and bought and bought and bought where they could buy, and destroyed where they could not buy!

Now, gentlemen, I and everyone here agrees with Mr. Byrnes as to what we want to accomplish—honest administration, reasonable rates and efficient service. We all agree on that. And what we want to do, we who oppose the merger, is this: we not only want to do what Mr. Byrnes desires in that respect, but we want really to enable him to accomplish his other desire—that he be not burdened now with this northern system of railroads—that he be not burdened with that, but that he be allowed to work out, with his associates, with all the ability and all the capital that they can raise, the great and many problems which the New Haven Road now has. Therefore, we desire legislation not only to take that away from the New Haven which it has acquired without authority under our law, but to prevent such a disposition of that stock as would result in a complete transportation monopoly and would also give to Massachusetts control of the monopoly itself.

Now, Mr. Byrnes puts to you as the danger, as what might happen, the impotency of New England in regard to what exists west of the Hudson River. If the New Haven had spent upon a line west of the Hudson River one-half of the money which it has spent and the obligations which it has incurred in subjecting to absolute monopoly all of southern New England, we should in New England be independent if the New Haven is independent! One hundred and fifty more millions of dollars of New Haven money and obligations have gone into forging the chains of monopoly on southern New England. It was not necessary to own all the trolleys in Rhode Island and Connecticut and in southern Massachusetts and in southern New York State. It certainly was not necessary to do it at a price by which their late trolley acquisitions in Connecticut stand at $153,000 a mile of track—there are roads in Rhode Island that stand at $142,000 per mile of track—when we in Massachusetts cannot earn reasonable dividends upon roads constructed at a cost of $48,000 per mile of track. That money that has gone into those acquisitions, and into the steamship lines, would have built us a trunk line, not to Buffalo, but to Chicago, and the whole of the West would have been open to us.

But they had *not* the desire to supply New England. Their desire has been, and their theory has been, that the thing for the New Haven to do is to possess control of the transportation in the New England states.

Now, the question for us, is there hope in that? Is there prospect in that of relief from the present situation, and hope for the future? It rests, and rests wholly, upon this idea that the railroads may be trusted for their enlightened self-interest to do what is best for the community.

We in America have found out that in spite of the extraordinary ability of railroad managers, the community must look out for itself, just as the community must look out for itself in other ways. It had to look out for itself in the matter of insurance, and all the insurance men said that the community knew nothing about insurance. The politicians thought the civil service reformers knew nothing. The municipal government of the city of Boston probably thought that the Finance Commission of Boston, and those that desired it, knew nothing. The community must protect itself, and the people of Massachusetts today must exercise their reasoning powers.

Mr. Mellen tells you that he is going to give us, if he gets this huge power, better rates between northern and southern New England. I say, in the first place, that we may judge the future by the past. Mr. Byrne has told you some things that he said occurred in his presence. I may tell you some things which occurred before the time he came to New England. He has spoken of this differential of five cents on Western lines which they want to preserve to us. Before he came, and before the New Haven controlled southern New England as it controls it now, we had a differential not of five cents, but of ten cents, and the New Haven compelled our northern railroads and our differential route South at a time when the Merchants & Miners was still free from New Haven control—it compelled them to reduce that differential from ten cents to five cents. By that line—the Old Colony Road today—in spite of the promises of what we were going to receive—freights on the New Haven went up, instead of going down, and freights of all the differential roads were raised five cents, that is, from a differential of ten cents to a differential of five cents.

We have heard just that sort of siren song before. "Men may come, and men may go," and this very delightful personality that we have with us tonight, representing the New Haven, Mr. Byrnes, may go as he has come, but the monopoly goes on forever if once it is started. Remember that. And remember also that just this sort of talk as to the value of being a great, or part of a great system, was the thing that we erred in eight years ago, when we were going to have our commercial greatness established by being the great terminal of the New York Central Railroad. There is an instance, and there is an object lesson, which you have got to bear in mind; and side by side with the object lesson of the Boston & Albany lease is another object lesson, the object lesson of the Fitchburg, because, to a very great extent, the defects of the Boston & Maine Railroad as they exist today, the lack of financial elasticity, and the lack of improvement during the last six or seven years—I mean of such improvement as we had a right to demand of our transportation system—is due, in very large measure, if not wholly, to that Fitchburg lease. And why? When that Fitchburg lease was taken over, and we were going to have there too the benefits of this consolidation, what happened? The dividend on the preferred stock, seventeen millions and more of preferred stock, was increased one per cent, more than $170,000. The common stock, a large part of which was held—five millions of which was held—by the Commonwealth, paid no dividend. That was converted into a 3 per cent bond—seven million dollars in all—about two hundred thousand dollars. Then when the preferred stock went up the taxes went up. You have a fixed charge on the Boston & Maine as a result of that lease which means $400,000 a year, the equivalent of ten millions of dollars, which might have been expended in the improvement of that road. Think what that would have meant, gentlemen! Ten million dollars in improving the Fitchburg Railroad! We should have had admirable service in the Fitchburg Railroad if we could have spent upon it ten million dollars, and earned besides what those improvements would have brought to us on the Fitchburg. And when you come to this proposed merger, as it is euphemistically called—monopoly, as it should be called—when we come to that, gentlemen, it is introduced with a new charge of $300,000, the equivalent of about eight million dollars, which might be invested in improvement, because—see here!—Mr. Byrnes may be right that very large blocks of stock were owned outside and were turned over to the New Haven in exchange for New Haven stock, but you know—every man here must know—many stockholders, and large stockholders, exchanged their Boston & Maine stock for New Haven stock. And why? Because they were going to get eight per cent where before they got seven per cent; and that difference of one per cent, which upon the thirty million dollars of stock of the Boston & Maine means

$300,000, because the stockholder was going to get a return, means that the shipper has got to bear that charge, and also means, and has meant in the case of Boston & Maine, that improvement which would otherwise have been made cannot be made.

Now gentlemen, when Mr. Byrnes tells you that if they do not get the Boston & Maine, he fears for the independence of the New Haven. We fear, and we think that fear is well grounded today, that this movement to acquire northern New England, the railroad system of northern New England, is a device of the trunk lines, not to get the New Haven, which they already exert an extraordinary influence over, and in which they already have large holdings of stock, but to get northern New England, and to deprive us of that little independence we have, which is due wholly to the existence of two Canadian lines, The Grand Trunk and the Canadian Pacific, which these gentlemen, by community of interest, who control the trunk lines, and we believe control the New Haven, are trying to obliterate. That is the competition which has made New England as free as it is now. That is the competition which these trunk lines, through the New Haven's movements, wish to rob us of. And it is that independence which is all that is left to us since the New Haven has taken that other liberty which we did have until recently, through the Merchants & Miners Transportation Company, to send our freight via Baltimore and Norfolk to the West and to the South.

Now, gentlemen, do not be misled by any ideas that this is an age of consolidation, and that the manifest destiny is to be all consolidated. If Mr. Byrne's arguments were true and sound, they would prevail equally for the whole of the United States. We might as well have one railroad system for the whole country, because, for certain purposes, if the railroads do not want to co-operate, all railroads have junction points somewhere, and it is a question of whether they want to co-operate or do not. But, gentlemen, remember this: a consolidation may be a good thing, or it may be a bad thing. A combination may grow more efficient, or it may grow less efficient, by growing larger. We have seen one combination, one trunk line, with which the New Haven is very closely associated by traffic arrangements, but which is held up by now as a thing that they fear apparently—the New York Central—we have seen how that line has grown so inefficient that the Boston & Albany, which ten years ago was held up in this country as the model railroad, so that the Chicago, Rock Island & Pacific had emblazoned upon its banner "The

Boston & Albany of the West"—under this mania for consolidation, and the being a part of a through line which would give us the benefits of all those good things west of the Hudson which Mr. Byrnes wants us to have, it reached the degree of degradation that there is hardly a man in Massachusetts that has not suffered from it.

Don't imagine either, gentlemen, that there is such a thing as an efficient regulation where you do not have an efficient instrument. Our Massachusetts Railroad Commission has long had the reputation of being the best Railroad Commission in the country, as it was the first to be inaugurated. Our Commission has been absolutely powerless even to prevent the constant deterioration of the Boston & Albany Railroad. That ought not to be a very serious problem, to prevent deterioration. But the prevention of deterioration is not what we want—the prevention of deterioration merely. We want improvement. We want progress. We want men to think and men to feel and men to care for Massachusetts and to develop it.

Mr. Byrnes says the New Haven is a Massachusetts road; that we own 40 per cent of the stock and 60 per cent of the securities. Gentlemen, there is nothing so humiliating in this whole situation as that fact which he mentions, because although we do own 60 per cent of the securities and 40 per cent of the stock nearly, we are absolutely powerless so far as the New Haven is concerned. Of 24 directors in the New Haven, Massachusetts, with its great ownership, has two and the influence of those two, I venture to say, is not in proportion to their numbers.

Now, gentlemen, do not be misled by these generalizations which you have heard. Do not be misled, above all, by the charming personality of Mr. Byrnes, because Mr. Byrnes is not the New Haven Road. Mr. Byrnes has the great merit—he has many merits, and one of them is that he was born in New England; but he is not the New Haven Road, and we must remember the past of the New Haven—the past in fastening monopoly upon all the territory that it controls. We must remember its political past, and bear in mind that if this monopoly is once perfected, Massachusetts cannot control [it] under any circumstances. Massachusetts will be a state within a corporation, as Connecticut is now a state within the New Haven, and as New Hampshire has been a state within the Boston & Maine.

## 14

# Monopoly a Failure

*This is a transcription of a speech Brandeis gave sometime in 1913 where he talks about how poorly the New Haven Railroad has performed after all its acquisitions. The speech originally appeared in the August 1913 issue of* Business America.

The decline of the New Haven is of more than local significance. It teaches a lesson of national importance.

In most instances of monopoly, men have guessed and prophesied and philosophized as to what would be the results of certain practices which they saw beginning. Whether they were right or wrong would appear a generation hence; their children or their grandchildren would know, but they themselves would not see the outcome. In the case of the transportation monopoly in New England, the thing has all begun, developed, and come to its fruition under the observation and at the hands of men living throughout the process.

In 1903, the New Haven was properly recognized as one of the most sound and prosperous railroad properties in the world. It had an unbroken record of prosperity covering a generation. Then it entered upon an aggressive policy of monopolization, and in the course of ten years practically every desire of the management in acquisition of competitors was carried out. Neither state nor federal laws appeared to restrict them in their plans of expansion. The supply of new capital was unlimited.

At the close of the ten-year period, we have a property of greatly lessened efficiency, of weakened stability and markedly impaired prosperity.

During nearly all this time, the country has been exceptionally prosperous, and the property has had a management which has been generally accepted throughout the country as embracing the best financial brains and experience of America. To what can the failure be due in the main except to the adoption of a fundamentally fatal policy—the policy of monopoly, which removes all tests of efficiency and all incentive to efficiency—a policy which involved the creation of a unit of such excessive size that the possibility of efficient management was removed?

The decline of the New Haven was due to a disregard of inexorable laws. First, the fundamental law of business, which has recognized the need of competition as an incentive to efficient action; second, that fundamental law of human nature which recognizes the limitations of man, namely, that there is a limit to the amount or number of things which any man or body of men can accomplish or do well; third, the inexorable law of arithmetic by which two and two will always make four, despite reports of presidents and financial advisers who insist on stretching it into five.

The New Haven management has disregarded likewise other laws. It ignored the laws of Massachusetts, which prohibited it from acquiring trolley lines in that state and the Boston & Maine Railroad stock; laws which prohibited the issue of many of the bonds and stocks that have come on the market. The company proceeded in its process of monopolization as if Congress had never passed the Sherman Anti-Trust Act and as if the Supreme Court had never rendered the Northern Securities decision.

About seven years ago, it was charged that the New York, New Haven & Hartford Railroad had violated the law of Massachusetts in acquiring ownership of trolley lines in that state. Governor Guild sent a message to the Legislature calling attention to the matter, and a bill was drawn designed to compel the New Haven to relinquish the trolley lines. Officers and counsel of the railroad protested that the New Haven had a broad charter from the state of Connecticut, under which they believed they had a right to do what they were doing. They asked that Massachusetts refrain from legislation, and, instead, have its Attorney General bring a test case in the state courts to ascertain their rights. Members of the Legislature insisted that, at the rate at which the New Haven was then acquiring trolleys, it would have all the Massachusetts lines by the time the case could come to final adjudication. The New Haven officials were very indignant at this suggestion and Charles F. Choate, its counsel, under Mr. Mellen's direction, gave a written promise that there would be no further acquisitions pending the outcome of the proceeding. To avoid the possibility of future misunderstanding, an inventory of their holdings and of those contracted for was furnished the Legislature. Massachusetts took the New Haven at its word. The Legislature adjourned in July without action on this matter. In October, the Attorney General brought a *quo warranto* proceeding, as agreed, and carried it on with all diligence. By the way, the preceding Attorney General, Parker, had in two opinions declared the acquisition illegal.

Nine months later, we learned that, in the interval, the New Haven had, in defiance of its promise, proceeded to acquire a working control of the Boston & Maine, and also five more trolley lines in Massachusetts. Thereupon the Legislature enacted a law designed to operate as a temporary injunction and requiring the matter to be submitted to the State Railroad Commission for investigation and report—if the proposed merger was to be proceeded with. Such an investigation would have meant public hearings, which the railroad did not want. The management went instead before the Commerce and Industry Commission, whose jurisdiction was extremely doubtful, but where they could have private hearings.

About this time the question arose whether there had not been a violation of the Federal Anti-Trust law, as well as of the state law. I prepared a brief from that point of view, which I submitted to the United States District Attorney, and which was doubtless transmitted by him to the Attorney General of the United States and thence to President Roosevelt. At the end of ten months—in May 1908—a suit was brought under the Sherman law, by direction of the President. In the same year the Massachusetts court, in a unanimous opinion, decided that there had been a violation of the state law. But scarcely had Mr. Taft become President (in April 1909) when Governor Draper, of Massachusetts, sent a message to the Legislature practically advocating the Boston & Maine merger, and recommending legislation to ratify what had been done. The Legislature was so perfectly "in line" that the bill passed without the slightest amendment. And on the very day that the District Attorney was moving for the setting of a date for taking up the anti-trust suit, Attorney General Wickersham dismissed the suit against the New Haven. The merger seemed in great favor, and without opposition, passenger rates were raised, the New Haven and Boston & Maine increasing revenues $1,700,000.

Now, to go back a little, I had always regarded the New York, New Haven & Hartford as on a par with the Bank of England in point of stability. But the investigation into the facts made while preparing the brief for the United States District Attorney raised a doubt whether the management was not already straining the New Haven credit. Four months were spent investigating that question, and I reached the conclusion that the New Haven could not afford to buy and develop the Boston & Maine. These conclusions were embodied in a pamphlet in which I insisted the New Haven should cut down their dividends and should undergo a period of abstinence to get over the effects of its financial debauch, for the New Haven had already acquired a substantial monopoly of transportation in New England—having control not of railroads only, but steamboat lines and trolleys—some of them in New York state.

You must understand that 48 per cent (numerically) of the New Haven stockholders were residents of Massachusetts. The New Haven was *the* trust stock of New England; held by estates, widows and orphans. It sold on a 4 per cent basis, being exempt from taxation. (In Massachusetts corporations are taxed directly, and the stock in hands of holders is exempt.) The Boston & Maine stock also was very widely distributed for similar reasons.

See what has happened to these innocent investors: The Boston & Maine had never passed a dividend since 1844. It had sold as high as 195. Now it is about 59. The New Haven dividends had been at least 8 per cent since the consolidated corporation was formed in 1872; the stock had been as high as 252; now it is about 105.

Ever since public attention was directed to the facts in 1907 and 1909, there has been a campaign of lying and suppression. Finally, the investigation of the Interstate Commerce Commission dragged the facts authoritatively into the light.

But the fundamental weakness of this great monopolistic structure began soon to show itself. The company was overloaded with work and did it badly. It was overloaded with obligations, and income was deficient. The management didn't dare to cut dividends; that would have been concession of failure. So, it began to cut expenses. It dismissed men and cut off trains. All through 1911 this process continued. It had its natural result. You know the story of incessant complaint against poor service, and of recurring accidents. The complaints of shippers and the traveling public brought on, in the spring of 1912, the investigation by the Interstate Commerce Commission, and its decision has cleared the air.

The story of the New Haven should be an object lesson to those who have believed in the monarchical principle of business, who believe that the business thinking and financial guidance of the great enterprises of all the country can safely be committed to a few men. The New Haven management has been continuously in the undisputed control of a few men—J. P. Morgan & Co. and those of whom they approved. All the operations of the company were physically within a territory of close proximity to this seat of power. Nothing could have occurred which should not have been within the knowledge of these leading directors.

And yet within a period which has been marked by its freedom from vicissitudes of business, the most prosperous and stable of our railroad properties has fallen into decline—a decline obviously attributable to a gross mistake of fundamental policy, intensified by a series of serious mistakes of judgment involving many millions of dollars. Does not this history of the New Haven show that a continuation of concentrated control of our enterprises by the few financial leaders is bound to impair our industrial and financial efficiency?

15

# Price Fixing

*This is a transcription of a speech Brandeis gave to the Associated Advertising Clubs of America on June 11, 1913. While trusts often used price fixing as a means of freezing out their competitors, Brandeis argues here that it could be used as a way of keeping those companies in business. A typescript of the speech is kept in box 235 of the Brandeis papers at the University of Louisville. It has never been published before.*

Mr. President, ladies and gentlemen: It is fitting that you busy men should pause at times to take, as it were, an account of stock; to compare the condition and the progress in your own individual business with that of other men in your particular trade or line, and that you should take the broader view even and compare your own individual affairs with that of business in general. And when you look upon this, the business ago, the business of the last decade, the business of the last generation, the one significant fact that impresses itself on all hands is the fact of growth; growth, in the first place, in the position which business holds in the world's activity. It fills a larger place today relatively in the life of the nation than it ever has before. Evidenced as you see it, not only by the constant trend to growth in the cities as compared with the country, but with the fact that in each and every city a larger and larger proportion of the people are engaged in business activity, involving as it does the invasion of 7,000,000 of American women into the domain of industry. And that growth is manifesting itself by the fact that to a greater and greater extent the high ability of the nation is finding in business a proper field for the exercise of its power. Not only in scope. Of course, in volume the evidences of growth greet us on all sides. They appear to the eye. They appear to the student of statistics in the growth of exports and in that constant and even more significant growth of the import of raw material. They greet us in the weekly study of the bank clearings with figures so huge as to remind us of those with which we undertake to describe the distances of the heavenly bodies from one another. But far more significant than the growth in volume is the growth in the character of business, the growth of dignity, the growth which perhaps may be best described by that gradual conversion of business into a profession. Because what does a profession mean? What are the distinguishing characteristics of a profession from any other occupation? I take it the distinction is mainly this: A profession is an occupation for the successful pursuit of which preliminary training, intellectual in character, involving knowledge, involving learning as distinguished from skill, is essential to high success. A profession, in the second place, is an occupation pursued not wholly for him who pursues it, but also for the benefit and service it will be for others. And in the third place, the distinguishing characteristic which I think you will find as applied to every profession is this: That excellence in the profession and the degree of excellence are measured not by the amount of money which the person who pursues the profession earns from it. Large earnings come with almost any profession, relatively large to the minister and the teacher and the sociologist, as well as the architect and the lawyer and the physician, provided he excels, because there is such a demand for efficiency in this world, and the supply is so small, that he who possesses it in a gainful occupation cannot fail to get the benefit of it in money.

But no one would think of measuring the ability of a minister, the eloquence of the eloquent gentleman who has just preceded me, by saying what his salary is as compared with that of another, any more than he would undertake to measure the ability of a social worker or a professor or a doctor by saying what his earnings have been during the previous year. The test of ability is excellence of performance. It is the ability of doing things better than they have been done by others. It is the ability to advance the particular line of human activity to which the man is committed.

I believe that the course which manifests itself so clearly in the professions is manifesting itself to a greater and greater extent each year in business. And it is necessarily so, because business is a very different thing from what it used to be. It involves knowledge in a way that it never did before. You have it evidenced by the fact that all of our great universities, Harvard, Dartmouth, the University of Illinois and dozens of others are instituting their schools of business. And it is necessarily so, because see what the complexity of business is. Everywhere science invades it. We have had mechanical and electrical science, and latterly, the science of management; and not only that, it invades the great questions of dealing with men. Sociology—dealing with multitudes—is the most difficult of all problems in business today. It requires a training and a study entirely different from what they were years ago.

Passing from that, we come to the great problems of the relations with the public, which involves questions merely of statesmanship rather than the ordinary questions of a few years ago—shrewdness in the making of a bargain. With that has come this ennoblement of business. There has come a change. See what it is! I take it, it is manifesting itself principally in three ways. The first is by the entrance of truth as a maxim of business; that for which your Convention stands preeminently. Think of the situation of business even a generation or less ago. Trade talk? What did it mean? Trade talk, translated into English, meant lying. The attitude of the community, the attitude of the law towards persons trading with one another, was to regard them as engaged in a contest of wits, with very few rules of the game to cover the contest. The law, in all its solemnity, had very much the same impartial and sympathetic attitude to those engaged in bargaining together that the Western wife had toward the husband when she said, "Go it husband, go it bear." That was the attitude of the law. Nothing that was said, however untrue, and very little deceit, was any cause of which the law took cognizance. And why? Because the law said it was unreasonable to expect the purchaser to believe the things that the seller said in regard to his goods. No reasonable man would believe, and therefore, in pompous language, following the Latin, they said "Let the buyer beware." They had even an idea that that had a social and economic significance. On the other hand, they regarded the buyer as a man who ought to, at his peril, find out all the defects and the faults in the article which he purchased. See how we have advanced beyond that doctrine!

And what is the second great advance that is so closely allied to the first? It is introducing to business the idea of service, the idea of value. A generation ago the idea of a bargain was a transaction in which one person got the benefit of it to the disadvantage of another. The idea today of a bargain in business is a transaction in which both sides receive the benefit. The old idea of trade in the past, with its secrecy, with its insincerity, with its taking advantage of the other person when we got a chance, was an equation of two unknown quantities, and today it is an equation of two known quantities.

The third great idea which has made its way into business is that of fair quality. The very idea of old bargaining of getting all you could from a person, regardless of the value of your article was, that possibly no two people would be treated alike. The idea today which has found its way into business is equality of treatment as an absolute essential to business. That idea made its way first through the public service corporation, where discrimination as between members of the public or different customers was recognized as being a far more serious evil even than extortion of rates, and that idea, the great truth, as to equality of treatment, a great democratic truth that has found its way now into general business is what we have today. One of the greatest advances which business has made in the last generation or more has been the advance to the one price store. That was a huge advance, an advance in labor saving, an advance in conscience saving, a huge advance making possible big business in the truest sense of that word.

There we found, in the one price store, the giving of value, the telling of truth—we found in those the advances of business to a higher plane, and to a dignity beside that of the learned and old professions. Man came to value, and to value in a peculiar way, those things which would signify truth and value and quality of treatment and fairness. They developed the trademarked goods, the proprietary goods, they developed those and as they carried out that development, the guarantee of truth, the guarantee of value and securing to each prospective customer an equal treatment, there developed also, necessarily, with the merchant the one priced goods: the goods that are to be sold not only to his immediate customer, the jobber, at one price, but are to be retailed throughout the country at one price to whoever should buy them. No doubt that movement is the movement to truth and the movement to value. It has its origin wholly, perhaps, or mainly, at all events, in ethical arbitration on the desire for righteousness. But it is one of those happy facts in this world that righteousness and truth are in entire accord with what is best for man. The business could grow, could develop as other American businesses have developed, only upon the things consistent with truth and with necessity and the highest ethical standards.

So, ladies and gentlemen, you have been developing in a perfectly natural order this one price, this price protected article, just as we have the one price store and just as we have value giving and the striving to give value rather than to get as much as you can and give as little as you can in the bargain. But the law said, "Let the buyer beware." After the business world had learned that that was no way to do business. The law has been laggard in recognizing the value of these one price articles which have become common in recent years, and which should become far more common if we are to carry out this idea of giving value and getting it in a transaction. Think what it means to have an article guaranteed, a trademarked article, and a guarantee as to price! See what bargaining would be and what business would be if you had a variation not only in the value of the article which you are selling and the quality of the article that you are selling, but in the money you are getting for it. That is the condition among primitive people—a shifting and doubtful currency. The greatest advance in business and the one thing essential to great business was to have a stable currency. It was labor saving, time saving: it made a multitude of transactions possible and enabled people to transact business through a large number of agents and agencies and employees. Exactly so it is in regard to the one price article. It moves on; it makes business possible; it helps to make business ethical, because you gentlemen know as no audience could better know in this country, the cutting of the one price article by individual concerns is done almost exclusively for no legitimate purpose. It is consistently said that the fixed price is out as a leader. I think it would more accurately represent the fact to say that it is out as a mis-leader.

It undertakes, inferentially, to make the customer believe that this article, which is being sold at ten, twenty, or thirty per cent below its standard value, represents the rate of bargain or discount which he can hope to get on any goods which he buys in any store. And you know that that is not so. It is unethical. The fault with the courts in refusing their sanction to the effort to protect that worthy service of keeping the selling price standard and stable is that they have failed to study, failed to acquire all the facts. More than that, the decision which has been rendered in recent years, denying protection to the one price article has another and very significant result. It is through the association of price fixing that monopolies exist. People knew that the Standard Oil Company fixed prices by agreement; that the Steel Trust fixed prices; that the Tobacco Trust fixed prices; that the Sugar Trust, in some way or another, fixed prices; and this idea of anything that fixed prices being objectionable and being against the public interests, created an atmosphere which permeated the courts and which led them to stamp as illegal anything in which the attempt was made to fix a price or protect a price. And the distinction is, of course, when we come to think of it, perfectly clear. On the one hand, you have a combination of individuals forming a monopoly, a capitalistic monopoly, and fixing the price of a standard article by reason of that monopoly. On the other hand, you have an individual man or concern in a competitive line of business undertaking to maintain his creation, that which is his property, which he has contributed to the world, through his effort, intellectually and his character, to put it out in the world in the form which he believes is essential to a fair distribution among the people. That fixed price article, or the one price article, in the competitive business is the greatest protector of competition there is. It stimulates competition, and the man who fixes this price, fixes it knowing that if he fixes it too high that either one of two things happens. Either people will not buy, or if they do buy, if his profits are large, a score of competitors will come in the market with him. That distinction between the one price competitive article, is entirely in line with the ethical development of business, and it is going to be and must be differentiated most clearly from the fixed price in monopoly; and it is your business gentlemen. It is the business of you men who are engaged in the advertising of articles who understand this, who know it, to bring that education to the whole people to make them realize that, as I stated, the cut price article, is a misleader, and it leads not only to cutting the throat of the manufacturer, but the individual retailer. Make that clear to people when you talk to them, and make it clear to them, also, that if this one price article is really to be suppressed—as I do not believe it can be—if that system were to be suppressed, it would result in the fostering of monopoly and of the great capitalistic combinations in a way that it has never been done before. It would substitute the mail order house and the great chain of stores with the hundreds of thousands of retail dealers over the land, because man would say with the manufacturers, "We cannot protect our own creation, unless by combination." And this price protection, this misunderstood protection, instead of being inconsistent with the public welfare, as you all know, it is the greatest protection to the small man, the small dealer, to the jobber, to the individual manufacturer who is endeavoring to put his ability and his character in the work of his life.

There, gentlemen, is a specific task which rests upon you, and it is happily, as I said, a task within the line of ethical development of business; a task which is in harmony with the idea of the profession of business and of raising merchandising and manufacturing to a dignity equal to the highest and noblest profession.

16

# Twin Evils of the Literacy Test

*This is a transcription of a speech Brandeis gave to a number of Congressmen on April 6, 1915, at Boston's New Century Club in response to Woodrow Wilson's vetoing of a bill that would have required all immigrants to pass a literacy test before being admitted into America. The speech was printed in the April 15, 1915, issue of* La Follette's Magazine.

We men of Massachusetts have come together in honor of her representatives in Congress and others because they have done honor to the Commonwealth and to the nation. By supporting our noble President, they have averted a disaster; they have helped to maintain the policy of courageous generosity, which has made America great, and which has served well the cause of liberty and humanity.

We, who are gathered here, know how strong are the arguments against the Literacy Bill. But let us not misconceive the situation. We are celebrating not a victory, but an escape. The danger remains. We have "scotched the snake, not killed it." It will recover from the blow; it will rise again to renewed effort, and perhaps with greater strength. If we wish to protect our country from threatened danger—from the lowering of high standards involved—we too must be active, and we must be united. Effective defense demands above all things that we should perceive clearly the twin evils which are concealed under the cloak of the literacy test.

FIRST: *The evil of privilege*. This immigration bill is not a literacy bill. It is an exclusion bill. It wishes to prevent others from sharing in the blessings which our country offers. If this measure had been one to ensure the advance in the United States of literacy or education, then surely the people of Massachusetts would be united in its favor. From the time when the Pilgrim fathers, landing from Holland, brought with them our common school system, up to this day, when our forward-looking Governor is working for university extension, the voice of Massachusetts has been emphatically and continuously for the spread and improvement of education. No state in the Union, no country in the world, appropriates for education as much per capita as does Massachusetts. Massachusetts was the leader not only in the movement for free schools, but also in the movement to make attendance upon free schools compulsory. So closely has Massachusetts associated education with citizenship that it led also in making literacy a condition of the right to vote; and although Massachusetts has of all the states nearly the largest percentage of inhabitants of recent foreign descent, it has also the smallest percentage of illiteracy. The opposition of the great majority of the people of Massachusetts to the literacy test arises not from a failure to appreciate education, but from a recognition of its true value. Education is a means, not an end. Education is beneficent if used as an instrument of liberty—as a means to worthy ends; and as our President said, literacy is a test not of character, but of opportunity.

The protest of Massachusetts men against the Burnett bill is a protest against the sway of privilege—against the closing the door of opportunity. Practically every man now coming to this country lacks that rudimentary education prescribed by the Burnett bill, lacks it by reason of misfortune, not of fault—the misfortune of oppressive laws like those of Russia where the Jewish children are to a large extent excluded from the schools; or the misfortune of poverty resulting from past oppression, like that of Southern Italy, or the Balkan Peninsula where it had been impossible to extend the advantages of education. Under the Burnett bill, those who live in countries free and prosperous, where education is universal, are to continue to enjoy the opportunity of immigrating to America; but those who are in dire need by reason of present or past oppression are to be denied the existing opportunity of bettering their condition. Surely, here is another instance where "to everyone which hath shall be given; and from him that hath not, even that which he hath shall be taken away from him."

SECOND: *The evil of race discrimination.* The vice of the exclusion movement is even more serious. It is not an accident that the test imposed by the restriction bill is literacy. The purpose of the bill was to restrict immigration from the Mediterranean and southwestern Europe. Literacy was adopted as a test because it was known that many of those people whom it was desired to exclude could not pass it. The movement thus springs from the conception or claim of race superiority. It involves necessarily race discrimination and must lead to race antagonism. How dangerous such conception of race superiority becomes, the present war bears witness. The world is beginning to recognize that a lasting peace cannot come until this arrogant claim of race superiority shall have been abandoned; because the claim of race superiority is certain to be followed by the attempt of one race to dominate over the other.

Strange indeed is it that Americans should seek to foster this idea; for racial equality is the complement of democracy. Democracy rests upon two pillars: One, the principle that all men are equally entitled to life, liberty, development, and the pursuit of happiness; and the other, the conviction that such equal opportunity will most advance civilization. Aristocracy on the other hand denies these postulates. It rests upon the principle of the superman. It willingly subordinates the many to the few, and sacrifices the individual, insisting that civilization will be advanced by such sacrifices.

The aristocratic theory applied to peoples led to Russianizing Finland, and to Prussianizing Poland and Alsace. And the British Alien law teaches us that even in a country where liberty has long been established, the assumption of race superiority leads to discrimination against "aliens" already admitted. Thus, by the English literacy test he only can now be naturalized who reads and writes and speaks the English language.

America, dedicated to liberty and the brotherhood of man, rejected heretofore the arrogant claim that one European race is superior to another. America has believed that each race had something of peculiar value which it could contribute to the attainment of those high ideals for which it is striving. America has believed that in differentiation, not in uniformity, lies the path of progress. Acting on this belief, it has advanced human happiness, and it has prospered.

The present movement for discriminatory immigration restriction runs directly counter to these noble traditions. It has sought to make the accident of birth, not character or merit, the test whether the applicant for admission is a desirable citizen. Once before—more than half a century ago—America, forgetful of her ideals, yielded to the selfish cry of America for Americans, and founded the Know-Nothing Party, which demanded, among other things, that no foreign born should have a vote until after twenty-one years' residence in America.

Swept by the craze, Massachusetts elected a Know-Nothing Governor. It is among the few blots upon her 'scutcheon. That year is one which men of Massachusetts have tried hard to forget. The gentleman from Essex County, in supporting immigration restriction, does not represent the Massachusetts of today, nor the noble Massachusetts of history. He not only bears the name, he embodies the spirit of that Know-Nothing Governor whom the Commonwealth quickly repudiated.

17

# A Speech on Suffrage

*This is a transcription of a speech Brandeis gave on October 12, 1915, at the Tremont Temple in Boston on the importance of women getting the vote. A typescript of this speech is kept in folder NMF 47-3b of the Brandeis papers at the University of Louisville. It has never been published.*

The demand for equal suffrage is supported by two powerful arguments: the right of woman to have her full share in determining the conditions under which she and her children shall live, and the duty of woman to bear her full share of responsibility for the conditions of the community. That women should enjoy this right and perform this duty is essential to the success of democracy.

This need of the state seems to me the strongest argument for equal suffrage. The state requires of women that fuller development which can only come through the assumption of broad responsibilities, and it requires the help which only women so developed can give. My own conversion to suffrage came through experience—through finding that in the public work in which I took part, the aid of women was not only most effective, but at times indispensable. We who believe in democracy are convinced that no class or section of the community is so wise or so just that it can safely be trusted to govern well other classes or sections. This is largely because of the limit of our understanding—our contracted vision.

The general welfare demands, therefore, of each class and section of the community (if not indeed of each individual), that contribution which it alone can make—the better understanding which comes from familiarity, from intensity of interest, from being persons directly affected. In public works with which I have been engaged, involving efforts at social and economic betterment, I have found that the contribution of women was peculiarly valuable. It was a contribution which men could not or at least did not make. It embraced deep understanding; a recognition of true values; deep devotion and singleness of purpose.

The widespread change in attitude towards woman suffrage today as compared with a generation ago, does not represent so much a change of opinion as a change of conditions. There has come about through quiet evolution in the past generation a change in the functions of government, and in the condition of women, so vast that if it had come suddenly, it would have been recognized as perhaps the greatest of human revolutions. Little more than a generation ago we led distinctly individual lives. The function of the state was mainly the preservation of order among these individual units. The state concerned itself only to a slight degree with individual families. Today the state is in a certain sense one large family. We have come to recognize that in a democracy everyone is affected by what every other person does, and that to protect each from harm, each must become his brothers' keeper. Just as we established in our cities rules for fire protection, laws to prevent contagion, and laws to ensure the purity of food—matters previously left to the discretion of the individual household—so we have undertaken, through the power of the state, to ensure, to a certain extent, the proper bringing up of the family. We compel school attendance. We prohibit the labor in store and factory by small children. We prevent the sale to them of cigarettes. We limit likewise the hours of labor of women. And even for adult men, we prohibit by factory laws and by tenement house laws, the working or living under conditions deemed unsafe or unsanitary.

In connection with all of these matters, woman has done great service. Women's function is still the care of the family and of the home. But the family and the hours which demanded her attention have grown, while the duties of woman in her individual family have been much diminished by the woolen and cotton mills, which released her of spinning; by the ready to wear garment manufactures, and the hosiery mills which relieved her largely of sewing and knitting; the preserving and canning establishments, and the prepared food establishment which relieved her largely of work incident to cooking. By reason of smaller families, or not marrying, the great social changes which have attended the industrial revolution have brought duties to the larger house, and the larger family, demanding of her exacting attention, and for these she has been fitted by the gradual change in her condition and occupation. She has been fitted for these new duties, or rather, for the new application of old duties, partly by what is called higher education, and to a far greater degree by her participation in the industrial life of the nation. The women in industry—the 7,000,000 wage earning or salary earning women of the country, receive a training which fits them for the problems of government, just as well as do the occupations of men. Some of the problems of government they are not adapted for, but that is also true of men. This is but an instance of the fundamental truth upon which democracy rests: that the general welfare can be attained best by cooperation of all classes and sections of the community—by each contributing what it can do best. Men and women will supplement each other here in the political world as they do in other departments of life, if only the opportunity is given. This surely they have done in suffrage states.

Of women's ability to bear her fair share of the common burden, no observer of life during the past generation should doubt. Indeed, they have shown great aptitude specifically in things political. Can anyone find in the political life of this commonwealth finer work of organization or more public-spirited devotion than that exhibited by the women in the present campaign?

18

# What Loyalty Demands

*This is a transcription of a speech Brandeis gave before the New Century Club in Boston on November 28, 1905—the 250th anniversary of the settlement of Jews in the United States. Brandeis uses the occasion to discuss the responsibilities of citizens living in a democracy. A typescript of the speech is held in box 235 of the Brandeis papers at the University of Louisville.*

It is fitting that the period of national Thanksgiving should have been selected for commemorating the two-hundred and fiftieth anniversary of the arrival of Jews in America. A great people whose history for 2000 years presents an almost unbroken record of persecution has found here a welcome. The blessings of a noble civilization—itself the fruit of generations of self sacrifice—have been extended in a spirit of brotherhood and with generosity unparalleled.

It seems proper on this occasion to consider the obligation which this great privilege of American citizenship involves—the obligation of loyalty to American institutions and ideals. What does such loyalty demand?

In the first place, loyalty demands complete democracy—the elimination so far as humanly possible, of class distinctions. In a country whose constitution prohibits discrimination on account of race or creed, there is no place for what President Roosevelt has called hyphenated Americans. There is room here for men of any race, of any creed, of any condition in life, but not for Protestant-Americans, or Catholic-Americans, or Jewish-Americans, not for German-Americans, Irish-Americans, or Russian-Americans. This country demands that its sons and daughters whatever their race—however intense or diverse their religious connections—be politically merely American citizens. Habits of living or of thought which tend to keep alive difference of origin or to classify men according to their religious beliefs are inconsistent with the American ideal of brotherhood and are disloyal.

In the second place, loyalty demands from the individual citizen a life consistent with the character and purposes of our institutions. Free government cannot endure, the purposes for which it exists cannot be attained, except among a people honest, courageous, intelligent and just. While we may not in America discriminate between men because of differences in race or creed, we must distinguish clearly between the honest and the dishonest, between the pure and the corrupt, between the just and the unjust, between the man of public spirit and him who is steeped in sordid selfishness. The dishonest, the corrupt, the unjust, the selfish are hostile to the American ideal of brotherhood and are disloyal.

In the third place, loyalty demands of every citizen active participation in government. Of him who has most in ability and intelligence, most is required, as the rich should contribute most in money to the expense of government. Few have the privilege or the burden of serving the state in an elective or an appointive office, but nearly every male inhabitant holds by birth or naturalization the office of citizen, and as such has the right and the obligation to vote. Every voter is a member of the government, is one of our country's rulers. The proper performance of the duties of that office is essential to the welfare of the state. These duties are not simple. They are difficult and exacting: for it is not sufficient that men vote—though even that formal duty is neglected by nearly two-fifths of our citizens. It is essential that men vote right. In order that the voter may rule properly, he must seek accurate information about men and measures. He must seek to distinguish between the good and the bad—between the genuine and the sham—between the demagogue and the statesman. Above all, he should recognize the seriousness of this office of citizen, the seriousness of the vote which is its expression. He may not cast it out of fear or favor or be influenced merely by friendship. He may not cast it lightly. He should remember that he holds the power which inheres in his vote as a sacred trust to be exercised for the common good, and that he who selfishly omits to cast it, as he who casts it selfishly—is disloyal.

Such is the loyalty demanded of an American: and lives so led are also the truest expression of loyalty to the noble traditions of the Jewish race. Through energy, perseverance, self-restraint and devotion, guiding large intelligence or genius, men of Jewish blood have, wherever opportunity permitted, taken rank among the foremost in almost every branch of human activity. They have achieved much in the material world—but their greatest triumphs are spiritual. Prone to idolatry, they had power within themselves to hurl from its pedestal the golden calf. Lovers of ease, lovers of pleasure, lovers of money, they had power within themselves to save their souls by lives of austerity.

As Professor Butcher has beautifully said in his Harvard Addresses: "To the Hebrews it was committed to proclaim to mankind the One and Supreme God—to keep alive His pure worship, to assert the inexorable moral law in a corrupt and heathen world.... Disencumbered of material greatness, they enlisted themselves on the side of purely spiritual forces. It was their prerogative 'to be an ensign to the nations'—to bear the banner of the true God. And long after the Jewish state had fallen, their religion became 'that of civilized humanity.'"

The unity of God involved the brotherhood of man. "Ye shall have one manner of law for the stranger as for one of your own country" declared its code. For as the demands of Jewish law "knew no restrictions of race, so its privileges were open to all."

The recognition of these high ideals of the Jewish race its members found at last in America. Loyalty to them is loyalty to true democracy—loyalty to the American ideals of liberty, fraternity, justice.

## 19

# The Harvard Law School

*This history of the Harvard Law School was published in the January 1889 issue of* The Green Bag.

The much-debated question, whether the law school or the lawyer's office affords the better opportunity for legal training, may well be considered settled. Undoubtedly each offers advantages which the other does not possess. All lawyers concede that a short apprenticeship in the office of a practitioner is valuable; but a thorough knowledge of legal principles is essential to higher professional success, and this knowledge, which under all circumstances is difficult of acquisition, can rarely be attained except as the result of uninterrupted, systematic study, under competent guidance. For such training, the lawyer's office seldom affords an opportunity. That this is now the prevailing opinion among lawyers is shown by the growth of law schools in the United States, and the introduction in England of systematic instruction in the common law, both at the universities and at the Inns of Court.

It is but a century since the first school for instruction in the common law was founded. The Harvard Law School, the oldest of all existing institutions devoted to such education, is scarcely seventy years old. Its age, the eminence and ability of its instructors and the excellence of its methods made it a potent factor in the struggle to establish the value of school training. Now that the battle has been won, it may be interesting to consider the condition of legal education at the time the Harvard Law School was founded, and the development of the school itself.

The elaborate system for acquiring a knowledge of our law, which prevailed in England at the time of the settlement of the colonies, and which Lord Coke has so graphically described in his preface to the Third Reports, fell into disuse there soon after his time. In America nothing similar ever existed. There was little need of lawyers in the early days of American life when the barrister was apt to be regarded as a barrator. But during the movement which culminated in the independence of the colonies the law became more and more a subject of general interest. Already before the Revolution, Blackstone was found, it is said, side by side with the Bible in the houses of laymen. With a growing respect for the knowledge of the law, the lawyers grew rapidly in number and importance. Still, no means had been provided of training the aspirant for the bar. Here, as in England, the student learned what he could by reading and re-reading the few textbooks then existing, by listening to the conversation of lawyers, and by watching the proceedings of the courts. After his admission to the bar, the young lawyer doubtless learned, as he does now, by that most expensive method of instruction—his own mistakes.

Professor Greenleaf describes the method of study which he and Judge Story pursued as follows: "We both commenced the study of the law many years since, amidst the drudgery and interruptions of the lawyer's office, perusing with what diligence we could our Blackstone, Coke, and other books put into our hands." This sort of legal training, which may have been adequate at a time when the scope of the common law was narrow and the reported cases comparatively few, naturally proved itself inefficient when the commercial development of England and America brought with it a corresponding increase in legal principles and in litigation. The inadequacy of such training was particularly obvious in the United States, where the varying decisions rendered in the different states—grafted as they were upon the English stock—had resulted frequently in a less homogeneous development of the law. The evils of the existing means of legal education being greater in America and the conservative force of tradition less, it is natural that the reform should have been inaugurated here. Even prior to the organization of the Harvard Law School in 1817, systematic instruction in the common law had been given in America. A professorship in English law is said to have been established at William and Mary College in Virginia as early as

1782. In 1790 a law professorship was established in the College of Philadelphia, and James Wilson—one of the Associate Justices of the Supreme Court of the United States—was appointed the first professor. Judge Wilson prepared a series of lectures designed to cover three courses. The first was delivered in the winter of 1790–1791, and a part of the second course was delivered the following winter. In April 1792, the College of Philadelphia and the University of Pennsylvania were united under the name of the latter; a law professorship was created in the new university, and Judge Wilson was appointed to fill the chair; but for some reason no lectures on law were delivered there for many years. Judge Wilson's law lectures were published in 1804—after his death. These early professorships cannot be considered as in any sense establishing law schools or separate departments of universities. Besides, like the law schools at Litchfield, Connecticut, and Northampton, Massachusetts—the early competitors of the Harvard Law School—they were soon abandoned.

The school at Litchfield, which was the first regular school for instruction in the English law, was founded by Tapping Reeve, author of the treatise on domestic relations. When, in 1798, Mr. Reeve was appointed Associate Justice of the Superior Court of Connecticut (of which bench he subsequently became Chief Justice), Hon. James Gould, author of the work on "Pleading in Civil Actions," took an active part in the management of the school. These gentlemen, together with Jabez W. Huntington, who became an assistant upon Judge Reeve's retirement, were the only instructors whom the school ever had, and in 1833 it was discontinued, after a life of fifty years. During most of that time the reputation of the school was high. In 1813, it was attended by more than fifty students, and the aggregate membership during its whole existence exceeded one thousand. It was what might be called a private school, for it was unincorporated, had no power to confer degrees, and was managed by the instructors. The method of instruction at Litchfield in 1831 is thus described in an official publication: "According to the plan pursued by Judge Gould, the law is divided into forty-eight Titles, which embrace all its important branches, of which he treats in systematic detail. These Titles are the result of thirty years' severe and close application.... The lectures, which are delivered every day, and which usually occupy an hour and a half, embrace every principle and rule falling under the several divisions of the different Titles. These principles and rules are supported by numerous authorities, and generally accompanied by familiar illustrations.

"Whenever the opinions upon any point are contradictory, the authorities in support of either doctrine are cited, and the arguments advanced by either side are presented in a clear and concise manner, together with the Lecturer's own views upon the question.

"In fact, every ancient and modern opinion, whether overruled, doubted, or in any way qualified, is here systematically digested. These lectures, thus classified, are taken down in full by the students, and after being compared with each other, are generally transcribed in a more neat and legible hand.... These notes thus written out, when complete, are comprised in five large volumes," etc. Mr. Huntington held examinations, every Saturday, upon the lectures of the preceding week, consisting "of a thorough investigation of the principles of each rule," with "frequent and familiar illustrations, and not merely of such questions as can be answered from memory without any exercise of the judgment." Mr. Reeve's lectures were accompanied by more of colloquial explanation. A Moot Court was held at least once in each week.

The school at Northampton was founded in 1823 by Judge Samuel Howe, who had once been a pupil at the Litchfield School, and his former law partner, Elijah H. Mills, a lawyer of extensive practice, and a United States Senator from Massachusetts. In 1827, Mr. Mills's law partner, John Hooker Ashmun, was added to the list of instructors. The prominence of Judge Howe and of Senator Mills, and the great legal ability of Mr. Ashmun gave the school a high reputation, but this, too, appears to have been in the strictest sense a private school. Its average attendance numbered hardly more than ten; and in 1829, when Mr. Ashmun accepted a professorship at Cambridge, the school was discontinued. The method of instruction adopted at Northampton seems to have resembled that at Litchfield. The professors read written lectures, of which the students were supposed to take copies, and there were less formal oral lectures and recitations.

The Harvard Law School had its origin in a gift of Isaac Royall, a prominent citizen of Massachusetts, who died abroad in 1781. In his will, made in England in 1779, whither he had gone after the battle of Lexington, Isaac Royall devised to Harvard College more than two thousand acres of land in Royalton and Granby, Massachusetts, "to be appropriated toward the endowing a professor of Law in said College, or a professor of Physic or Anatomy, whichever the Corporation and Overseers of said College shall judge best for its benefit; and they shall have full power to sell said lands and put the money out at interest, the income whereof shall be for the aforesaid purpose."

Had the College availed itself immediately of this devise, the school at Cambridge might perhaps have been organized before Tapping Reeve began his instruction at Litchfield Hill. But it was not until 1815 that the proceeds of this devise, which amounted then to $7943.63 and had hitherto remained in the treasury of the College unappropriated, were first devoted to the establishment of a professorship of law. The annual income of this fund, about four hundred dollars, was supplemented by the fees of students; and Isaac Parker, then one of the justices (afterwards Chief Justice) of the Supreme Judicial Court of Massachusetts, was appointed under the title of Royall Professor. This was, however, merely a college professorship, like the Vinerian professorship at Oxford, and the professorship of law at the College of Philadelphia. The foundation of the Harvard Law School, as such, dates from the year 1817, when Asahel Stearns was appointed University Professor of Law. The statutes of the College required him to open and keep a school in Cambridge for the instruction of the graduates of the University and others prosecuting the study of the law; and in addition to prescribing to his pupils a course of study, to examine and confer with them upon the subjects of their studies, to read to them a course of lectures, and to generally act the part of a tutor, so as to improve their minds and assist their acquisitions. His compensation consisted of the tuition fees paid by the students. Chief Justice Parker took but little part in the exercises of the school. His duties required him to deliver every summer fifteen lectures to the undergraduates and the members of the Law School; these lectures, which were necessarily general and elementary in their nature, related chiefly to the Constitution of the United States and of Massachusetts, and the early legal history of New England. In 1827 Chief Justice Parker resigned his professorship, and in 1829 his withdrawal from the school was followed by that of Mr. Stearns. The method of instruction adopted at Cambridge during this period appears to have resembled that which prevailed at Litchfield and Northampton. Mr. Stearns's treatise on "Real Actions," once widely known, embodies a course of lectures read by him to the students. Besides, there were less formal lectures, recitations, and Moot

Courts. In spite of the learning of Mr. Stearns and the eminent ability of Chief Justice Parker, the Harvard Law School was not successful during the early years of its existence. The belief in school instruction was still limited to a few, and most of those were attracted to Litchfield and Northampton. The former enjoyed a national reputation, and the latter, being situated within a hundred miles of Cambridge, was a dangerous rival. Thus, the Harvard Law School, notwithstanding the zeal of its professors and its connection with a college then already widely known, received but few students. The largest number until 1829 was eighteen, and the average attendance was only eight.

The year 1829 marks a new era in the life of the Harvard Law School. In that year Nathan Dane, a lawyer of Beverly, Massachusetts, author of the once famous "Abridgment of American Law," and the alleged draughtsman of the never-to-be-forgotten Ordinance of 1787 for the government of the Northwest Territory, following the example of Viner, gave to the school the profits of his Abridgment. This gift secured for Harvard the services of Joseph Story, and for the world his epoch-making treatises on the law. In laying the foundation for the professorship which bears his name, Mr. Dane prescribed that "it shall be the duty of the professor to prepare and deliver and to revise for publication a course of lectures on the five following branches of Law and Equity equally in force in all parts of our Federal Republic—namely The Law of Nature, The Law of Nations, Commercial and Maritime Law, Federal Law and Federal Equity—in such wide extent as the same branches now are and from time to time shall be administered in the courts of the United States, but in such compressed form as the professor shall deem proper; and so to prepare, deliver, and revise lectures thereon as often as said Corporation shall think proper;" and "as the Hon. Joseph Story is by study and practice eminently qualified to teach the said branches both in Law and Equity, it is my request that he may be appointed the first professor on this foundation if he will accept the same; and in case he shall accept the same it is to be understood that the course of his lectures will be made to conform to his duties as one of the Justices of the Supreme Court of the United States; and further, that time shall be allowed him to complete, in manner aforesaid, a course of lectures on the said five branches, probably making four or more octavo volumes, and that all the lectures and teachings of him and every professor so to be appointed shall be calculated to assist and serve in a special manner law students and lawyers in practice, sound and useful law being the object." The amount given was ten thousand dollars, and the fund was increased by a bequest of five thousand dollars upon Mr. Dane's death, a few years later.

Joseph Story became Dane Professor, John Hooker Ashmun was appointed Royall Professor, and the school entered upon a period of great prosperity. At the time Story assumed the duties of instructor at Cambridge, he was fifty years old. He had been for eighteen years Associate Justice of the Supreme Court, a position which he held until his death. This was a period during which the attention of the public was perhaps more generally fixed upon that tribunal than at any other in our history. The learning and the lucid exposition displayed in Story's judicial opinions had won the admiration of the bar throughout the land, and the opportunity of hearing his lectures was eagerly seized. Almost immediately upon his appointment as professor, the school changed its character from a local to a national school of law. It became broader in its aims; it improved in the quality of its instruction, and the attendance grew larger. When, sixteen years later, death severed Story's connection with the University, the Law School numbered one hundred and sixty-five students, representing nearly every State in the Union. During the same period the law library increased so rapidly that, after a few years, it surpassed any in America. Between 1829 and 1845, nearly thirty thousand dollars were expended by the Law School in the purchase of books, and it received in addition Samuel Livermore's collection of works on the civil law, which is said to have been the most valuable collection of its kind in this country. In 1831, Mr. Dane offered to advance funds to enable the College to supply a separate building for the Law Department. Dane Hall was erected in 1832, but the growth of the school soon necessitated extensive additions, which were completed in 1845. The prosperity of the school was so great that in spite of the purchases for the library and the enlargement of Dane Hall, there had accumulated at the time of Judge Story's death, a surplus of over fifteen thousand dollars. How well he had per formed the duty imposed by Mr. Dane to revise his lectures for publication may be seen from the fact that during this period Story published all his treatises on the law, filling no less than thirteen volumes.

Although it was the fame and ability of Story which then gave to the Harvard Law School its impulse and which established its national character, yet others contributed in no small measure to the high reputation which it won at this time. John Hooker Ashmun was a man of extraordinary legal acumen; and upon his early death, in 1833, Simon Greenleaf, then reporter of decisions for the Supreme Court of Maine, was appointed Royall Professor of Law. Greenleaf had already distinguished himself at the bar by his critical discrimination of legal principles, and for fifteen years he brought these mental faculties to bear with great effect upon his work as a teacher of law. In the performance of his duties as professor he prepared the work on "Evidence," which was published in 1842 and soon won for him a reputation in every country where the common law is administered. His learned edition of "Cruise on Real Property" appeared after he became emeritus professor.

The method of instruction prevailing at the Law School during this period was in many respects similar to that which had been practiced during the earlier years of its existence. Professor Ashmun's instruction was mainly by recitations adding informal explanations where it was deemed necessary. Judge Story taught mainly by lectures and resorted rarely to questioning students. Professor Greenleaf adopted the same method, with such difference only as the different qualities of his mind would naturally produce. The multiplication of textbooks on the lesser branches of the law—many of them prepared by the professors themselves—had done away with the careful copying of the instructor's lectures which at Litchfield and Northampton had occupied much of the students' time. A list of books for a course of study was prepared, and the students had an opportunity of airing their learning occasionally at the Moot Courts which were held by the professors.

Within a few years after Judge Story's death the school numbered among its instructors Hon. William Kent of New York, George Ticknor Curtis, Franklin Dexter, Luther S. Cushing, the author of the famous Manual, and Edward G. Loring. Henry Wheaton accepted the position of Lecturer on International Law but died before entering upon the performance of his duties. Later, Richard Henry Dana delivered courses of lectures. But Kent, Curtis, Dexter, Cushing, Loring, and Dana were lecturers for short periods only; and during the twenty years following the death of Greenleaf, the fame of the school rested upon the ability and zeal of Judge Parker, Theophilus Parsons, and Emory Washburn.

At the time of his appointment as Royall Professor of Law, Joel Parker, though but fifty-two years of age, had been for nearly fifteen years a member of the Superior Court of New Hampshire and for nearly ten years its Chief Justice. He will doubtless long be considered *the* Chief Justice of that state, for he was one of the ablest of American judges. Stored with the practical experience of a long professional and judicial life, patient, assiduous, and accurate, keen in argument and clear in exposition, he devoted for twenty years all his powers to the performance of his duties at the school.

Theophilus Parsons became Dane Professor of Law in 1848 and held that position until the year 1870. He was a son of the eminent judge whose name he bore—the Chief Justice of Massachusetts—and inherited from his father a deep love for the law, and a power of impressive statement rarely equaled. At the date of Parsons's appointment as professor, he was fifty-three years of age, and had acquired considerable reputation, both as a practitioner in admiralty and as a literary man. His fame, however, rests upon his work at Cambridge. The ability of fixing and holding the attention of students, which he possessed in an unusual degree, gave him a high reputation as a lecturer, and the treatises prepared by him in his professorial work soon spread his name far and wide. His "Law of Contracts," which appeared in 1853, is said to have had a larger sale, during the lifetime of the author, than any legal textbook ever published in any country. Like Story's and Kent's Commentaries, it was often quoted in England, and for more than twenty years it was the leading book of reference on the subject in America. A Kentucky law student, finding it constantly relied upon by the courts of his State, inquired whether there was any statute making it an authority. At comparatively short intervals between 1856 and 1869, Professor Parsons also published works on Mercantile Law, Maritime Law, Bills and Notes, Partnership, Marine Insurance, and Shipping and Admiralty. His reputation as a legal text writer became so extended that his publishers sold over one hundred and fifty thousand copies of his "Law of Business Men,"—a treatise on commercial law for laymen. It is believed to have netted the author, in royalties, fully $40,000.

In 1855, Emory Washburn, a lawyer of rare integrity and industry, who had attained prominence not only in his profession, but also as judge, legislator, and Governor of Massachusetts, was appointed lecturer at the Harvard Law School, and in the following year became University Professor of Law—a position which he filled for twenty years.

The name of the professorship was changed, in 1862, to Bussey Professor, a considerable fund then becoming available to the Law School from a bequest of Benjamin Bussey, Esq. Like his colleague, Professor Parsons, Washburn soon became favorably known both as a lecturer and as a legal writer. Probably no instructor at the Law School was ever more generally loved by his students. While at the bar, every client's cause had been his own; and as a professor he identified himself in the same manner with his pupils—their hopes and successes were his; their fears he sought to dispel by warm words of encouragement. His works on the American Law of Real Property and on the American Law of Easements, renewing their youth with each new edition by the aid of able annotators, are still the leading books of reference on those subjects in America.

During the twenty-five years following the death of Judge Story, the attendance at the school fluctuated considerably, owing partly to the war, partly to the competition of law schools which were organized elsewhere in large numbers, and partly, perhaps, to other causes. The highest number of students (one hundred and seventy-six) was reached in January 1860; the lowest (sixty-nine), in July 1862. In the year 1869–1870 the attendance at the school was one hundred and fifteen. The method of instruction during this period remained substantially the same as that which was practiced under Judge Story and Professor Greenleaf; namely, oral lectures illustrating and explaining a previously prescribed text-reading, with more or less examination thereon.

On January 6, 1870, Christopher Columbus Langdell became Dane Professor of Law—an event which, like Story's appointment, to the chair forty years before, marks an epoch in the history of the school and of legal education. In external conditions, two men could hardly have differed more widely than Story and Langdell at the time each entered upon his duties as an instructor of law. Story had a national reputation; at the early age of thirty-two he had been appointed one of the judges of the highest court in the land; he had been tendered the Chief Justiceship of Massachusetts; his official position, his family connections, and his social qualities had secured for him the acquaintance of the most prominent men of this country; he was the pride of New England; the University was honored when he accepted the professorship at the Law School. Langdell, on the other hand, was almost unknown; he had held no public office; at the bar of New York, of which for more than fifteen years he had been a member, not many could be found who had even heard of him; he had rarely been seen in the courts; in Boston there were few to whom his name was known. But some of the leaders of the New York Bar had discovered his ability, and there were some other lawyers of prominence both there and in Boston who remembered that, nearly twenty years before, there had been at the Harvard Law School a young student from New Boston, New Hampshire, of indomitable will, of untiring industry, and of a strong legal mind, who assisted Professor Parsons in his work on the "Law of Contracts," and acted for some time as librarian of the school. They remembered that their fellow-student had occupied himself much with the proper methods of study; they had regarded him then as something like a genius in the law; and when they heard that Mr. Langdell had been chosen Dane Professor, they did not share the anxious concern which other friends of the school expressed at the appointment of a man comparatively unknown.

As soon as Professor Langdell assumed his new duties, changes were suggested in the requisites for admission and for graduation, and in the methods, order, and quality of instruction, which being eventually approved by the faculty, completely revolutionized the school. Prior to 1875, no examination or particular course of previous study was prescribed as necessary to entitle one to admission to the school. As a result, the classes contained many students whose training had not been sufficient to enable them to profit by the instruction given. In that year requisites for admission were first prescribed, and since then no person other than a graduate of a college has been admitted without passing a written examination in Latin or French and in Blackstone's Commentaries. Persons not candidates for a degree, called special students, are still permitted to attend the school without examination. Likewise, prior to 1875, any person who had for three terms or eighteen months been enrolled as a member of the school was entitled to a degree without having necessarily attended a lecture or passed an examination. Under the new administration, the regular period of residence for the degree of Bachelor of Laws was first lengthened to two years, and subsequently a third-year course was added. Now this degree is conferred only upon students who have been in the school at least two full years as candidates for a degree and have passed examinations in the studies for the three years. The course of study itself has been greatly changed and enlarged. The amount of instruction given in the school previously to 1870 appears not to have exceeded ten exercises a week. Although the course actually covered two years, half of the course only was given at the school each year, so that it was purely a matter of chance whether the student began his studies with one or the other set of subjects. This arrangement doubtless proceeded upon the theory that "there is neither beginning nor end to the law, neither fundamental principle nor natural development." But with such a theory the new faculty most thoroughly disagreed. They believed that the law was a science and should be studied as such. And so, throughout the three years' course of study the subjects are arranged with reference to their fundamental character. The total number of exercises each week is now thirty-five. The following is the course of instruction for the year 1888–1889:

FIRST YEAR.

*Contracts*. Professor Keener. Three hours a week. Langdell's Cases on Contracts.

*Property*. Professor Gray. Two hours a week. Gray's Cases on Property.

*Torts*. Mr. Schofield. Two hours a week. Ames's Cases on Torts.

*Civil Procedure at Common Law*. Professor Ames. One hour a week. Ames's Cases on Pleading.

*Criminal Law and Procedure*. Mr. Chaplin. One hour a week. No textbook.

SECOND YEAR.

*Bills of Exchange and Promissory Notes*. Professor Ames. Two hours a week. Ames's Cases on Bills and Notes.

*Contracts*. Professor Keener. Two hours a week. Keener's Cases on Quasi-Contracts.

*Evidence*. Professor Thayer. Two hours a week. No textbook.

*Jurisdiction and Procedure in Equity*. Professor Langdell. Two hours a week. Langdell's Cases in Equity Pleading.

*Property*. Professor Gray. Two hours a week. No textbook.

*Sales of Personal Property*. Professor Thayer. Two hours a week. Langdell's Cases on Sales.

*Trusts*. Professor Ames. Two hours a week. Ames's Cases on Trusts.

THIRD YEAR.

*Agency*. Professor Keener. Two hours a week. No textbook.

*Jurisdiction and Procedure in Equity*. Professor Langdell. Two hours a week. Langdell's Cases on Equity Jurisdiction.

*Partnership and Corporations*. Professor Ames. Two hours a week. Ames's Cases on Partnership.

*Suretyship and Mortgage.* Professor Langdell. Two hours a week. No textbook.
*Constitutional Law.* Professor Thayer. Two hours a week. No textbook.
*Jurisdiction and Practice of United States Courts.* Professor Gray. One hour a week. No textbook.
[*Law of Persons.* Professor Gray. One hour a week. No textbook.] Omitted in 1888–1889.
*Wills and Administration.* Professor Gray. One hour a week. No textbook.
[*Conflict of Laws.* Professor Keener. One hour a week for half the year. No textbook.] Omitted in 1888–1889.
[*Points in Legal History.* Professor Ames One hour a week for half the year. No textbook.] Omitted in 1888–1889.

In addition to the foregoing third-year subjects, third-year students may elect any second-year subjects which they have not taken in their second year. Every student who has been in the school one year or more has an opportunity each year of arguing in a moot court case before one of the professors.

Every candidate for the honor degree will be required to take ten hours a week in each of the last two years. Every candidate for the ordinary degree will be required to take in the second year ten hours a week in the subjects of that year, and in the third year eight hours a week.

Great as have been the advantages derived from these changes in the requirements for admission and for graduation and in the quantity and order of the instruction, it is believed that Professor Langdell's chief contribution to the cause of thorough legal education was the introduction of an entirely new system of teaching law—a system which was at first looked upon with great distrust by his colleagues as well as by the bar, but which, making converts from year to year, has eventually established itself firmly at the school. Believing that law is a science and recognizing that the source of our law is the adjudicated cases, Professor Langdell declared that, like other sciences, the law was to be learned only by going to the original sources. It was there that the authors of textbooks had gained their knowledge of the law, and there only can others acquire it. No instructor can provide the royal road to knowledge by giving to the student the conclusions deduced from these sources; his chief aim should be to teach the student to think in a legal manner in accordance with the principles of the particular branch of the law. He should seek to inculcate and develop in legal reasoning the habit of intellectual self-reliance. The sphere of usefulness of the teacher of law according to this conception of his duty is not a narrow one. Having gone over the ground which the student is to traverse, the teacher can, in the first place, aid the student by removing from his consideration the great mass of cases on the particular subject which bore no part in the development of the principle under discussion. Eliminating those, he selects the cases especially worthy of study; and for the convenience of the student the select (not leading) cases on the different subjects are published as a collection. The principle upon which such a collection is made was thus stated by Professor Langdell in the preface to his "Select Cases on Contracts," which appeared in October 1871—the first book of the kind ever published:

"Law, considered as a science, consists of certain principles or doctrines. To have such a mastery of these as to be able to apply them with constant facility and certainty to the ever-tangled skein of human affairs, is what constitutes a true lawyer; and hence to acquire that mastery should be the business of every earnest student of the law. Each of these doctrines has arrived at its present state by slow degrees; in other words, it is a growth, extending in many cases through centuries. This growth is to be traced in the main through a series of cases; and much the shortest and best, if not the only way of mastering the doctrine effectually is by studying the cases in which it is embodied. But the cases which are useful and necessary for this purpose at the present day bear an exceedingly small proportion to all that have been reported. The vast majority are useless and worse than useless for any purpose of systematic study. Moreover, the number of fundamental legal doctrines is much less than is commonly supposed; the many different guises in which the same doctrine is constantly making its appearance, and the great extent to which legal treatises are a repetition of each other, being the cause of much misapprehension. If these doctrines could be so classified and arranged that each should be found in its proper place, and nowhere else, they would cease to be formidable from their number."

These books of cases are the tools with which the student supplies himself as he enters upon his work. Take, for instance, the subject of mutual assent in contracts. A score of cases covering a century, contained in about one hundred and fifty pages and selected from the English reports, the decisions of the Supreme Court of the United States, and the highest courts of New York, Pennsylvania, and Massachusetts, arranged in chronological order, show the development of its leading principles. Before coming to the lecture-room, the student, by way of preparation, has studied—he does not merely read—say from two to six cases. In the selection of cases used as a textbook, the head notes appearing in the regular reports are omitted, and the student, besides mastering the facts, has endeavored for himself to deduce from the decision the principle involved. In the classroom, some student is called upon by the professor to state the case, and then follows an examination of the opinion of the court, an analysis of the arguments of counsel, a criticism of the reasoning on which the decision is based, a careful discrimination between what was decided and what is a dictum merely. To use the expression of one of the professors, the case is "eviscerated." Other students are either called upon for their opinions or volunteer them, the professor throughout acting largely as moderator. When the second case is taken up, material for comparison is furnished; and with each additional authority that is examined, the opportunity for comparison and for generalization grows. When the end of the chapter of cases is reached, the student stands possessed of the principles in their full development. Having attended as it were at their birth, having traced their history from stage to stage, the student has grown with them and in them; the principles have become a part of his flesh and blood; they have *pro hac vice* created a habit of mind. Like swimming or skating, once acquired, they cannot be forgotten; for they are a part of himself.

One objection to this method of study, naturally presents itself: "How can anybody give the time to study the law in this elaborate manner? Either one must cover only a small field, or a lifetime must be given to the mere preparation for the profession." This objection was anticipated and an answer to it was given by Professor Langdell in the passage quoted from the preface to his "Select Cases on Contracts." Undoubtedly, the principles of the law are numerous; one might almost say innumerable. It has been said that there are nearly three millions of distinct principles. This may be true; yet the fundamental principles are comparatively few. These only need be acquired; once acquired, they will be found springing up everywhere. They are immediately recognized and located; they are the guideposts that point the lawyer unerringly to his destination, however numerous the cross-roads or alluring the by-ways. Besides, the progress through the cases, though at first slow, grows more and more rapid as the student progresses in the particular subject and becomes accustomed to this system of study. Furthermore, the particular principles of law thus gained represent but a small part of the total acquisition while studying the cases on one narrow subject. The courts, the judges, the pleadings, the practice, the arguments of counsel, have become real things. Again, though a case is selected because it illustrates one stage in the development of a legal doctrine, a dozen points not directly connected with that doctrine may be involved or suggested, and these the student either solves for himself or seeks to have explained. The points thus incidentally learned are impressed upon the mind as they never could be by mere reading or by lectures; for instead of being presented as desiccated facts, they occur as an integral part of the drama of life, of an actual lawsuit. Besides, the study of the cases does not exclude the study of the treatises. The animated discussions in the classroom induce the student to resort to every means of fortifying himself, either for his own instruction or in order to overthrow his adversary in discussion, be it professor or fellow student. This leads the pupil to independent investigation and the treatises which are always accessible are rarely neglected.

There could be no stronger proof of the excellence of this system of instruction than the ardor of the students themselves. Professor Ames, writing of the school ten years ago, said: "Indeed, one speaks far within bounds in saying that the spirit of work and enthusiasm which now prevails at the school is without parallel in the history of any department of the University." What was true then is at least equally true now. The students live in an atmosphere of legal thought. Their interest is at fever heat, and the impressions made by their studies are as deep and lasting as is compatible with the quality of the individual mind.

The testimony of the value of this system of instruction which is furnished by the zeal of the students is supplemented by the actions of the professors. Each instructor at the school is entirely at liberty to choose the method of instruction which most commends itself to his judgment. Several of the professors declined for many years to adopt the system introduced by Professor Langdell. Slowly it won its way. Actual experience overcame all doubts. Now that general method—varied of course in the manner and extent of application, according to the views of the different instructors—is almost universally adopted at the school. See what Mr. Justice Oliver Wendell Holmes, Jr., of the Supreme Judicial Court of Massachusetts, says of it:

"But I am certain from my own experience that Mr. Langdell is right; I am certain, when your object is not to make a bouquet of the law for the public, nor to prune and graft it by legislation, but to plant its roots where they will grow, in minds devoted henceforth to that one end, there is no way to be compared to Mr. Langdell's way. Why, look at it simply in the light of human nature. Does not a man remember a concrete instance more vividly than a general principle? And is not a principle more exactly and intimately grasped as the unexpressed major premise of the half-dozen examples which mark its extent and its limits than it can be in any abstract form of words? Expressed or unexpressed, is it not better known when you have studied its embryology and the lines of its growth than when you merely see it lying dead before you on the printed pages?

"I have referred to my own experience. During the short time that I had the honor of teaching in the school, it fell to me, among other things, to instruct the first-year men in Torts. With some misgivings I plunged a class of beginners straight into Mr. Ames's collection of cases, and we began to discuss them together in Mr. Langdell's method. The result was better than I even hoped it would be. After a week or two, after the first confusing novelty was over, I found that my class examined the questions proposed with an accuracy of view which they never could have learned from textbooks, and which often exceeded that to be found in textbooks. I at least, if no one else, gained a good deal from our daily encounters."

We Americans, who have given to modern England systematic instruction in the law, who enriched its law half a century ago with the ideas of Kent, Story, and Greenleaf, may feel some pride in the fact that the English now recognize the value also of Professor Langdell's contribution to legal pedagogic. In 1886 Gerard Brown Finch, Esq., Law Lecturer at Queen's College, Cambridge, after thoroughly examining the system of instruction prevailing at Harvard, introduced at Queen's College Professor Langdell's methods, and for that purpose published a selection of cases on the Law of Contracts.

But the time has passed when we need look to the enthusiasm of students or to the opinions of professors for evidence of the value of the new method of instruction. It is eighteen years since it was introduced. Those who have had an opportunity of putting the legal education thus acquired to a practical test are perhaps best qualified to speak of its merits, and almost without exception they pronounce in its favor. Mr. James

C. Carter, probably the leader of the New York Bar, has expressed in the strongest terms his belief in the new method of instruction:

"Now, is this method open to the objection that the study of cases is apt to make the student a mere 'case' lawyer? Not at all. The purpose is to study the great and principal cases in which are the real sources of the law, and to extract from them the rule which, when discovered, is found to be superior to all cases. And this is the method which, as I understand it, is now pursued in this school. And so far as the practical question is concerned, whether it actually fits those who go out from its walls in the best manner for the actual practice of the law, I may claim to be a competent witness. It has been my fortune for many years to have charge of a considerably diversified legal practice; and the most that I have had to regret is that it has overwhelmed me so much with mere business that I have had too little time for the close study of the law which my cases have involved.

"It has been necessary for me to have intelligent assistants, and I have long since discovered that most valuable aid could be derived from the young graduates of this school. I have surrounded myself with them, partly for the reason that I have an affection for the place, and also because I have found them in possession of a great amount of actual acquirement, and—what is of more consequence—an accuracy and precision of method far superior to anything which the students of my day exhibited."

That Mr. Carter's experience is shared quite generally, appears from the following statement by President Eliot, contained in his report for the year 1885–1886 to the Overseers of Harvard College:

"It is good evidence of the value of the full three years' course that for several summers past the school has been unable to fill all the places in lawyers' offices which have been offered it for its third-year students just graduating. There have been more places offered, with salaries sufficient to live on, than there were graduates to take them."

The intellectual self-reliance and the spirit of investigation which this new method of instruction engenders, have produced the *Harvard Law Review* and greatly developed the Club Courts. The *Harvard Law Review* is a monthly journal of law, of the same general plan as the *American Law Review* and is managed wholly by the students. It contains articles also by the professors and others and is a magazine of high order. The Club Courts, which are practically Moot Courts, conducted entirely by students, have far outstripped in usefulness the Moot Courts held by the professors. These clubs have generally two sets of members, the junior court consisting of eight members selected from the first-year class, and the senior court consisting of nine members selected from the second-year class. The junior and the senior courts meet at regular intervals, and at each sitting a case is argued by two of the members as counsel, the rest sitting as judges. In the junior court, a member of the senior court sits as Chief Justice. The cases are regularly presented upon the pleadings; briefs are prepared, arguments made, and opinions—sometimes in writing—delivered by each of the judges. The cases are prepared with quite as much thoroughness as any work that is done at the school.

In material prosperity the school has also progressed steadily during the past eighteen years. The number of students has risen from one hundred and fifteen in the year 1869–1870 to two hundred and twenty-five in the year 1887–1888. The national—indeed the international—character of the school has been fully maintained. Since the establishment of the three years' course ten years ago, thirty-five states, two territories, and the District of Columbia, England and four of her provinces, Japan and the Hawaiian Islands have been represented at the school. The library now contains twenty-three thousand volumes and is believed to be in some respects the best equipped law library in America. About $3,000 is spent upon it annually. In 1881, Mr. Edward Austin gave the school over $140,000 for the erection of a new building, Austin Hall, which it now occupies. In 1882, the school received a gift of $90,000 to endow a professorship, and in the same year large gifts were made toward a library fund.

The enthusiasm of the graduates of the school found expression, in 1886, on the occasion of the celebration of the 250th anniversary of the founding of Harvard College. The Harvard Law School Association was organized, on Sept. 23, 1886, "to advance the cause of legal education, to promote the interests and increase the usefulness of the Harvard Law School, and to promote mutual acquaintance and good fellowship among the members of the Association." All former members of the school are eligible for membership in the Association. Its general meeting was held at Cambridge on November 5, 1886. The membership of the Association now numbers eight hundred and eighteen. For the current year it has made a gift of $1,000, to increase the instruction in Constitutional Law, and another of $100, for a prize essay to be competed for by members of the third year class. Similar grants for these purposes are to be made by the Association yearly.

In describing the progress of the school since 1870, we have referred only to the work of Professor Langdell. Those who have had any knowledge of the school during this period need not be told to how great an extent its prosperity should be ascribed to the co-operation of others who from time to time have been members of the faculty. Of none of the instructors is this more true than of the present professors, who have devoted themselves to the cause of legal education with never-flagging zeal. The tact and good judgment which they have displayed in dealing with the difficult problems of administration, and the ability—nearly approaching genius—with which they have put the new method of instruction into practice, have alone made it possible to carry through the changes at the school, and to obtain the moral and financial support from without which have brought the school to the high degree of prosperity which it now enjoys.

After Judge Parker's resignation, Nathaniel Holmes, formerly one of the justices of the Supreme Court of Missouri, was appointed Royall Professor; and later, Charles S. Bradley, formerly Chief Justice of Rhode Island and a lawyer of great ability, became Bussey Professor. During this period Edmund H. Bennett, N. St. John Green, John Lathrop, Benjamin F. Thomas, and New England's greatest lawyer, Benjamin R. Curtis, were lecturers at the school. O. W. Holmes, Jr., held a professorship for a short time before his appointment to the Supreme Bench of Massachusetts in 1883.

The *Catalogue of the Students of the Law School of Harvard University, 1817–1887*, which was prepared by John H. Arnold, Esq., its efficient librarian, under the inspiration of the Harvard Law School Association, contains five thousand two hundred and sixty-three names. A glance at its pages will show to how great an extent men prominent in public and professional life have received their early training at this school. Among those now holding offices under the federal government may be mentioned the Chief Justice and Mr. Justice Gray of the United States Supreme Court; the Secretaries of War, of the Treasury, and of the Navy; Senators Evarts, Hoar, Eustis, Chandler, and Gray, who will soon be joined by Senators-elect Walcott and Higgins; the Chief Justice and Mr. Justice Davis of the Court of Claims; Walter L. Bragg of the Interstate Commerce Commission; Judge Cox of the Supreme Court of the District of Columbia; the United States District Judges, Ogden Hoffman of California, Addison Brown of New York, Henry B. Brown of Michigan, Edward C. Billings of Louisiana; and, of the territorial courts, Judges Twiss of Utah, and Knowles and Blake of Montana.

On the highest state courts the school is represented in Maine, New Hampshire, Massachusetts, South Carolina, West Virginia, and Iowa, by the Chief Justices, and in New York, Rhode Island, Delaware, and Ohio, by associate justices. Five of the seven judges of the Supreme Judicial Court of Massachusetts were students at the school.

To the Dominion of Canada the school has furnished the present Minister of Finance, Charles H. Tupper, as well as judges, and many members of Parliament; and to the Hawaiian Islands, the Chief Justice and Judge M'Cully of the Supreme Court.

We should expect to find the names of leaders of the Boston Bar now, as in the days of Rufus Choate, among the former students of the Harvard Law School; and in other cities the school is no less ably represented than there. Take, for example, New York, with James C. Carter, William M. Evarts, Joseph H. Choate, William G. Choate, George Hoadly, George Frederick Betts, George De Forest Lord, C. C. Beaman, D. H. Chamberlain, and George Bliss; at Providence, Benjamin F. Thurston, and formerly Charles S. Bradley; at Detroit, George V. N. Lothrop, the late Minister to Russia; at Savannah, Alexander R. Lawton; at St. John (New Brunswick), Ezekiel McLeod.

The educational influence of the Cambridge school has not been confined to the instruction given within its walls. Former students have as professors of law elsewhere spread wide its teachings. Thus, Francis Wayland, the Dean of the Yale Law School, and Professor Simeon E. Baldwin, and Edmund H. Bennett, Dean of the Boston University Law School, studied at Cambridge.

Widely, too, has the Harvard Law School made its influence felt by the legal writings not of its professors merely, but also of others who were once its students. The last decade alone has given us, among others, Judge Holmes's work *The Common Law*, Langdell's *A Summary of the Law of Contracts*, Gray's works *The Rule Against Perpetuities* and *Restraints on the Alienation of Property*, Jones's treatises on Mortgages and Liens, Benjamin Vaughan Abbot's various writings, Pierce on *America Railroad Law*, Gould on waters, Thompson & Merriam on juries, Morawetz on private corporations, Merwin's *The Patentability of Inventions*, Stimson's

*American Statute Law*, besides the valuable writings of such authors as Preble, Austin, Grinnell, Aldrich, Wald, and Chamberlayne.

Among the many former students at the Harvard Law School who became prominent in spheres other than the law, may be named Caleb Cushing, Charles Sumner, Wendell Phillips, Rutherford B. Hayes, and Robert T. Lincoln; Elihu B. Washburn, Richard H. Dana, and Anson Burlingame; Motley, Prescott, and Parkman; James R. Lowell, William W. Story, and Dr. Oliver Wendell Holmes.

The Harvard Law School has done a great work in the past. May we not venture to hope that the work of the future will be immeasurably greater?

# 20

# Memoir

*After Woodrow Wilson nominated him to the Supreme Court in January 1916, Brandeis began a behind the scenes public relations campaign. Part of that campaign included dictating his life story to his secretary, Alice Grady. Portions of the dictation were used in a June 4, 1916,* Boston American *story titled "Boyhood of Brandeis." But the original document has been kept in the archives at Brandeis University, where it escaped the notice of Brandeis scholars until it was reprinted in the 2018 issue of the* Journal of Supreme Court History *under the title of "Notes for a Lost Memoir of Louis D. Brandeis."*

*This document reveals many details about Brandeis's life that were previously unknown, particularly about his education in Germany, his early days as a lawyer in Boston and how he got involved in public service work. Given the circumstances of its creation, this document is not a polished piece of art. Brandeis jumps back and forth in time and it ends with him free associating the names of the partners who joined his law firm. In addition, the first page of the document is missing so that it starts in the middle of a sentence that describes how his parents came to America. Regardless of these flaws however, it is an illuminating look at Brandeis's life.*

*I have added footnotes to identify many of the people Brandeis mentions.*

. . . they were all in a state of upheaval from the revolution, and they finally decided to settle at Madison, which was on the Ohio River, halfway between Cincinnati and Louisville in Indiana. It was expected to be a great city because it was the terminus of a railroad that ran from Madison through Indianapolis towards the northwest.

In September 1849, my mother Frederika Dembitz, to whom my father had been engaged before he left Prague, came over with her father, who was a physician, and her brother, who was afterwards a lawyer, Lewis Dembitz, and this large body of relatives and others, which included also the grandfather of Mrs. Brandeis.[1] They all went together and settled in Madison, and my father went there, and in a certain sense became a guide for the community, and left his business connections in Cincinnati.

My mother's mother was from Prague. She was a Wehle. And her father was a native of Pressburg in Austria. He was born in 1797. He was a physician, a graduate of Konigsburg in Prussia. He practiced in the eastern part of Prussia. My mother was born in Prussia and met my father when she was visiting her grandparents and her relatives in Prague.

My grandfather Dembitz traced his ancestry back to the Portuguese Jews who were expelled from Portugal at the time of the Inquisition and went to Holland and settled in Amsterdam.

In 1851, my father moved from Madison to Louisville, and shortly after coming to Louisville entered into the wholesale grain business, which he carried on for many years, a very large business, called Brandeis and Crawford. They carried on that business from 1851 to 1872, when the firm was dissolved, at the time our family went abroad. After he came back from abroad, my father entered into the grain business again with my brother Alfred, who still continues it under the name A. Brandeis and Son. I have recently received a congratulatory letter from William W. Crawford, who is a grandson of the Crawford who was my father's partner.[2]

---

1. Adolf Brandeis (1822–1906) and Frederika Dembitz (1829–1906) arrived in Madison in 1849. Frederika's father, Sigmund Dembitz (1797–ca. 1888) settled in New Orleans. Frederika's brother Lewis Dembitz (1833–1907) became one of Louisville's leading lawyers. While Brandeis was a teenager, he changed his middle name from David to Dembitz to honor his uncle. "Mrs. Brandeis" was Brandeis's wife Alice Goldmark (1866–1945). Her grandfather was Gottlieb Goldmark (1802–1811).

2. Adolph Brandeis's partner William W. Crawford (1820?–1876) died four years after the dissolution of Brandeis and Crawford. His grandson was also named William W.

Father was one of the most respected men in Louisville; he had an extraordinary business reputation. He was a very good and successful businessman and was considered then, back in the sixties and seventies, one of the wealthy men of Louisville.

From the latter part of the sixties down to 1872, there was a readjustment after the war, which was very great in the territory in which my father was. He was gradually losing, his investments were shrinking, and he finally concluded that there was nothing he could do to stay that situation, and he was prevailed upon to go abroad, which he always wanted to do. He went abroad with his family, with the expectation of staying 15 months, seeing his old friends whom he had not seen since 1848, and introducing his family to Europe.

While he was abroad first came the Panic of 1873, which swept away a large part of his investments, leaving only his mortgages intact. At first, he didn't care to come back until the storm blew over, and then he couldn't come back because first one sister and then the other became ill. Amy was ill with typhoid. She had hardly recovered when Fanny was taken ill. As the result, all of us—with the exception of my brother Alfred, who returned home in September 1873 to go back into business clerking—stayed over there until May 1875.

My father had a very interesting experience. After having been called rich, instead of doing as most people do and lose their money quickly, it took about ten years to complete the readjustment. Things in which he had no part, and could not help, just practically wiped out everything he had except one or two equities in some real estate. And that went on until about 1879 or 1880. And then after he had lost everything, he began business again, and the rest of his life he was in comfortable circumstances, and never again had any business troubles.

This experience had for me, and I think for my brother, the greatest advantages, and I have attributed my own attitude toward money and life a good deal to the fortunate circumstances of my father's troubles, in a way. As a boy, I had everything that money could buy. We were not rich according to modern notions, but well off, and in that community were considered rich. But in the important years of my life, age 13 to 14 and

Crawford (1878–1944). The younger Crawford was a lawyer who earned his degree in 1901 at the University of Louisville Law School, which would later rename itself after Brandeis.

up to the time I became independent, I had to pass through the experience of having practically nothing. So that even in Germany, while I was in school there, I earned money by teaching English, and translating.

I went to the Harvard Law School on money lent me by my brother who was then clerking. And I earned while I was in the law school not only enough to pay that back and pay the rest of my way, but I had $1200 when I got out of the law school. I was paid $2.50 an hour for tutoring. I had some of the "crowned heads" of Boston as my pupils. One lesson that I gave here in Boston, I got $5.00 an hour for.

At that time, we had to give a bond for $400 to cover our tuition. I didn't know anyone to go on my bond. I was introduced to Jacob H. Hecht,[3] who said, "Of course I will go on your bond."

The first school I went to when I was six years old was a school kept by an English lady, named Mrs. Wood, together with her maiden aunt Miss Price. The next year I went to a school kept by a Mr. Knapp, a German, where there was some instruction given in German. After a couple years there was organized in Louisville what was called the German-English Academy, under the management of Knapp and Hailmann.

That was a school like the Knapp school, where German was taught as one of the studies. I attended that. These were all private schools. I attended these until I was 14 years old. Then I went to what is the Public High School. It was then called the University of Louisville.[4] It was what we should call a high school. That was in December 1870. I graduated at the third year of that with a gold medal. I was 15 years of age.

In August 1872, I went abroad with the whole family, intending to stay 15 months, but our stay was prolonged by the illness of my two sisters.

We went first to England, and then along the Rhine, then to Ischgl, a summer resort in the Austrian Alps. From there to Vienna. I intended to enter the Gymnasium in Vienna, but unfortunately, I failed to pass the examination. I then saw how little I knew as compared with what I needed to know. The result was that I took some private lessons and attended some lectures at the university. But the principal thing that I was

3. Jacob H. Hecht (1834–1903) was a prominent Boston Jewish businessman and philanthropist.

4. Brandeis's high school is now known as Male High School. For a short while in the 19th century, it was called the University of the Public Schools of Louisville. As a result, Brandeis always considered himself an alumnus of the University of Louisville.

doing was devoting myself to music and art and the drama and literature and seeing people.

My family had always been a cultured family. Music, art, and literature were the things they had been particularly interested in. My sister Fannie was a rather extraordinary musician. I myself played the violin for many years and was familiar with musical things. We spent a good deal of the winter on those things and then went in March to Italy. We stayed four months. That is where my sister got typhoid. We went from there to Switzerland, intending to go back to America in the fall. But the panic had come, and Amy wasn't well enough. So, we stayed, and my brother went back to America, and I went off alone to Dresden to go to school. I was then 16. The family was to follow later. I had a most interesting experience, because for the first time I was entirely on my own footing.

It was expected that I would go to one of the private schools, but after inquiring about things there in Dresden, I made up my mind I wanted to go to the public school. I had a couple of letters to certain persons in Dresden. One wasn't there, and the other I called on the first Sunday after my arrival. I put up at a little hotel, the Hotel Meissner, and then I went in the next day to see the gentleman to whom I had a letter, a German-American. I talked with him, and he told me about the school his sons were in, and about other schools. I made some other inquiries and made up my mind to go to the public school. He said he would take me there, but couldn't do it until Wednesday, because he was moving. Well, I said I had made up my mind, I couldn't wait until Wednesday and that I would go myself. So, on Monday morning, the first thing I did was to move out of the hotel and look for lodgings, which I found in the neighborhood of the school.[5] Then I circled around the school like a moth around the candle. I worked my way up into the room of the principal (called the "rector") who said he couldn't admit me into the school unless I should pass an examination. I didn't want to make a try at the examination. I said I thought I knew enough to get into the second class, called the Secunda.

"But," I said, "I can't pass the examination. I have been studying for 15 months very different things and under very different conditions, and it wouldn't be a fair test."

5. The Annen-Realschule.

Well, he said I couldn't do it without. But I talked quite a little with him, and he said, "If you will take some private lessons, it will be three weeks before the mid-year examinations, and you can take the examination then."

I concluded I would take private lessons in all of the different subjects in which he said I would have to perfect myself. Then what I would have to have besides that were a birth certificate and a vaccination certificate. I said I could provide the vaccination certificate by having someone look at my arm, and my presence was evidence that I had been born.

I took lessons from various professors and teachers in the school and worked about 13 hours a day for three weeks. The holiday came along and when the new term commenced, I slipped into that school, without having to try for an examination. Nobody ever wanted one. This was in the October term of 1873. At the end of six months, when it came to the Easter term, this school was going to interpolate an additional Secunda. It was a school which prepared for the Polytechnic. The highest class was a Prima. But they had an upper and a lower Prima, which were two years, but only one Secunda, and one Tertia. They were going to interpolate an extra Secunda, and they were going to divide that class, some to go into the Ober Secunda, and some to the Unter Prima. I was among those who went into the Unter Prima.

When it came to the next Easter term, 1875, I was pretty well recognized as the leader of that class. There were two other boys who stood about as well—the only other boys in the school who were Americans. They were the Harjes boys, nephews of the Drexel Harjes of Philadelphia, who used to be the Paris correspondents of J. P. Morgan and Company.

I have now a book which was presented to me as a prize for high standing in the school. They let me select the book, and I selected Becker's *Art.*[6]

It was while I was there in Dresden that I was earning some money by teaching English.

During that period, from 1873 to 1875, was our panic in America. Hardly a letter came to my father that did not bring news of more losses. The family was most of the time not in Dresden but were away on account of my sister's illness.

---

6. A. Wolfgang Becker, *Charakterbilder aus der Kunstgeschichte* (Leipzig: E. A. Seemann, 1869).

All of the rules were in a certain way relaxed on my account. The rule was that you had to live either in an accredited dormitory, or with your parents. I lived absolutely alone and never had any supervision. Nobody ever raised a question.

The rule was that you could never absent yourself unless you had an excuse or certificate from your parents. I was away—visiting my parents in fact—and was delayed even for an examination. The rule was never enforced with me. I had very good standing—particularly so with the rector of the school, who was a lover of English. His name was Job. He was a man of very great tact.

There used to be a rule of the school that you had to bow (take off your hat) to every teacher in the school whether you knew him or not. The Harjes boys and I, and a good many of the boys objected. The Harjes boys and I didn't choose to bow to all those teachers, some of whom we didn't know. One of these men made a complaint to the rector. The rector, in one of his discussions in class one day said, "It is strange how people sometimes go to a good deal of trouble to do what would come naturally. Now, you see the English very often have in their hats little holes to ventilate them. Now if they, instead of that, would like our people to be disposed to take off their hats to people, they would get better ventilation, even with the ordinary hat."

Nobody knew what it was in reference to except us boys, but after that we always bowed.

By the time I got through I was in the Ober Prime, but we concluded to come back to America in May. I didn't go back to the school but spent the latter part of March and April in the town of Blankenburg, where my parents had been living with my two sisters for about a year. There we stayed until May 5th, 1875, when we started back for America.

When I came my sister was somewhat recovered from her long illness but was far from well. It was deemed inadvisable for her to go to Kentucky. She came here [Boston] to stay with a young girl whom we had met in Vienna and who travelled with us through Italy—a young girl named Lillie Rogers who had gone as companion with the Morningstar family. She was the daughter of a man who was an assistant in the treasurer's office at the State House. She herself had worked for a year, I think, as clerk in the State House—a very charming girl. She was just about the age of my sister. Fanny went to stay with her. I brought her over here. It was just the end of May, about Decoration Day. That was the first time I had seen Boston.

We had met abroad in the winter of 1873 Ephraim Emerton, who was travelling over there and was at the same pension with me in Dresden. He was an 1871 man at Harvard and talked up Harvard tremendously, so I had an idea I would go there. When I came here, besides bringing my sister, I also came to look at Harvard to see what class I could enter. The friend of Lillie Rogers who came with her to meet us was Rufus K. Wood. And the friend at Harvard who took me around and showed me through was Charlie Lord, the great friend of Denman W. Ross, and the son of Mrs. Frances Lord—a charming fellow in the Class of 1875, of which Denman Ross was also a member.

My sister was at that time engaged to Mr. Charles Nagel.[7] He came on and I returned to Louisville. While I was in Louisville, in the summer of 1875, my father's financial condition proved even worse than it had seemed from a distance. So, I concluded that instead of entering college, I would go direct to the Law School. And I came back and studied through the summer more or less, with a view to the law, and at the end of the summer, came on here to the Law School.

Of course, I became very much interested in the law and was recognized pretty soon by a number of good men. I was elected into the Pow Wow Club,[8] which was perhaps the best law club, being composed mainly by Harvard graduates, the only exception being John Aiken, who later became Chief Justice of the Superior Court.

While I was at law school (it was a two-year course at the time), my eyes gave out in 1877 from overwork. I had also done a lot of tutoring. Shortly after that, the election came on. At that time, the rule was that the class elected six men to write the oration, and then the faculty was to select one man to deliver it. I led the class on the popular vote. Then the faculty felt itself in a desperate position. Because the law of the University provided that nobody could graduate who was not 21. The question came up, how could a man who was not 21 be the orator when he

7. Charles Nagel (1849–1940) would marry Brandeis's sister Jennie. Besides being a prominent St. Louis lawyer, he would become President's Taft's Secretary of Commerce and Labor.

8. The Pow Wow Club was a student organization that held moot court competitions.

couldn't get a degree? Professor Langdell[9] was terribly troubled. He really wanted me to have the oration, and he thought and thought and stroked his beard, but he couldn't do anything. Finally, he sent me to President Eliot[10]—the first time I had seen the President. He said, "The rule is that the orator is to be one of those who receive a degree. The law says that you can't have a degree before you are 21. You won't be 21 until November. Commencement is in June. I don't see, Mr. Brandeis, how you can be the orator."

It took about three minutes for him to decide that question. I thought, "There is an example of an efficient executive." I wasn't so sorry for it because I couldn't use my eyes much. I was tutoring, and I knew I couldn't write an oration without a great deal of work. So, I felt rather relieved—quite content to get a degree later—particularly as I was contemplating spending an extra year for a post graduate course at the college.

To my surprise, on the morning of Commencement Day, it was announced that a special vote had been passed, in view of the very high standing I had, that under a special dispensation I was to get a *cum laude* degree then.

As I remember it, Starbuck,[11] a Nantucket man had the oration.

My eyes were in pretty poor shape. I thought the summer would cure them. But instead of that, when I got back in the fall, they were worse off than they were in the spring. I went through with a good deal of tutoring. But I went on with my work, both of teaching and studying, by having readers. To a great extent I had paid readers. This trained my mind so that if I went to a course, I could carry the whole thing without writing it out.

I did quite a little studying with Mr. Warren,[12] who used to do the reading with me. We worked together. That summer most of my teach-

9. Christopher Columbus Langdell (1834–1906) was the Harvard Law School professor who developed the case method of teaching law.

10. Charles William Eliot (1834–1926) was the president of Harvard from 1869 to 1909.

11. Henry Pease Starbuck (1851–1918) would become a professor at the Columbia Law School.

12. Samuel D. Warren (1852–1910) was Brandeis's best friend in law school and eventual law partner. The two of them wrote the influential article "The Right to Privacy." His father ran the paper business S. D. Warren and Company, which made the Warrens one of the richest families in Boston.

ing had been in the law, but I had taught also Saunders Bradley, the son of Chief Justice Bradley of Rhode Island, the father also of Charles Bradley of Bradley and Angell—afterwards Edwards and Angell. I taught Saunders and was in Providence at Judge Bradley's all that summer, taking a cure by gradually building up my eyes. I was supposed to read three times a day, one minute each time, the next day two minutes each time, and so on. When I got up to reading something over an hour each time, then the eyes gave out again.

I came back and took pretty good care of myself—went up to the mountains and did a good deal of walking. When I came back, my oculist said he thought I had better give up the thought of practicing law, that I never would be able to use my eyes.

When I wrote my father that, he said, "Well, there is a great physician in New York, Dr. Knapp, a German oculist." This was in the fall of 1878—October. I was staying out at Cambridge, where I was proctor—29 Thayer Hall. I had been proctor there since the spring of 1877. It gave me a room free, and an opportunity to earn some money.

Then I went over to see Dr. Knapp, and he tried me out, and said, "Nonsense! What you need is to take care of your eyes. If you use them right, they will grow stronger, and if they hurt you, it won't do you any harm. But you have to use them with reason. Be a reasonable man. See that you get good light, under good conditions. Don't use the eyes unnecessarily and they will gradually grow stronger."

So, when that announcement came, I made up my mind to go to St. Louis. There had been a plan of my going, and I went on the agreement that I was to have a position in the office of Mr. James Taussig. He was one of the leading lawyers in St. Louis and was an uncle of Frank W. Taussig.[13] He was counsel at that time in large corporation matters. He was also one of the trustees of the Kansas, Pacific Railroad, which was in litigation at that time, in receivership proceedings. So, I went out there, lived at the same time at the house of my sister, Mrs. Charles Nagel. There had always been a thought that sometime I would go into partnership with Mr. Nagel. But I hadn't any more than gotten out there when Mr. Warren, who in the meantime had been in the office of Shattuck,

13. James Taussig (1827–1916) was a friend of the Brandeis family back in Europe. His nephew Frank W. Taussig (1859–1940) earned his law degree from Harvard in 1886 and his sister Jennie married Brandeis's brother Alfred.

Holmes, and Munroe[14] and wanted to start in business on his own account. He began early in the autumn writing to me to come back and join him.

Well, I didn't like St. Louis life very well, although I plunged right into it. I knew pretty much everybody after one winter. But it seemed to me to be a pretty crude life. There seemed to be an absence of culture. Also, I had malaria, which probably had a good deal to do with my dissatisfaction. I felt homesick for Boston and for Cambridge. Without making up my mind, I came on here to see whether I would settle here. This was in June 1879. I wanted to be sure of a living. At that time, I had offered to me a secretaryship to Chief Justice Gray.[15] This meant not a continuous job, but sitting with him five hours a day when he wasn't on the bench, in his intervals of time, while he was writing his opinions.

With that and the other opportunities afforded, it seemed pretty clear that I could make a living. So, in July—just after the Fourth of July—I made up my mind on the toss of a penny, as to whether I would go back to St. Louis or stay here. I decided to remain here, and in 1879 we formed the firm of Warren and Brandeis,[16] and begun business at 60 Devonshire Street.

We stayed there until 1889, when we moved to 220 Devonshire Street; then moved here [161 Devonshire Street] in 1904.

I was secretary to Chief Justice Gray that summer and tapering off into January or February the following year. It was the understanding that I would not go to him if it interfered with other things I had to do.

By the early part of 1880, I began to have a lot of business. In the first place, we had a certain amount of business here almost at once through S. D. Warren and Company and friends of Mr. Warren—Train Hosford and Company and a few other people, who on their account of their friendship for the senior Warren came in to us.

Then in 1880, I was called by ex-Chief Justice Bradley into an important case down in Providence, Rhode Island to write the brief. The senior lawyer in the case couldn't be expected to write the brief and the junior

14. Shattuck, Holmes, and Munroe was Oliver Wendell Holmes, Jr.'s (1841–1935) law firm. His partners were George O. Shattuck (1829–1897) and William A. Munroe (1843–1905).

15. Horace Gray (1828–1902) was the Chief Justice of the Massachusetts Supreme Judicial Court. He would later be appointed onto the United States Supreme Court.

16. The firm is still in business today under the name of Nutter, McClennen & Fish.

was busy in the legislature. And so, Judge Bradley wanted me to write the brief, a very important one, in the ... Woonsocket Company case.[17]

I worked on that brief day and night for about six weeks and wrote a very learned and very effective brief. When they came to consider the brief, they concluded that the man who wrote it would have to argue it. So, I went down there, and for four or five days we argued that case. That gave me a certain standing. There were other stages in the case where I was called upon to act. That was the start of my Providence practice that came later.

Shortly after that, James Taussig, with whom I had been in St. Louis, had a case here: a suit against the Illinois and St. Louis Bridge Company—a stockholders' liability case.[18] We brought that suit here. Russell and Putnam, the leaders of our Bar here, were the lawyers on the other side. And we succeeded in winning one suit in the State court, and once in the Federal court, before Judge Lowell, the father of the present John Lowell. We won on a demurrer in the State court sufficiently so that the defendants got frightened and settled. We got a good fee out of that. So that by 1881, through these connections, and those that Mr. Warren had, we already had a pretty good practice, and people began to come in.

I had my first case before our Supreme Court through Mr. Jacob H. Hecht, who brought me the case of the Hebrew Benevolent Association against a subscriber who had impudently refused to pay—*The United Hebrew Benevolent Association v. Benshimol.*[19]

I became acquainted in that way with the Supreme Court, the Federal court, and with the Rhode Island court. And very shortly after that, in 1881, Mr. Albert Otis got me to give an opinion on a matter connected with railroad litigation. The Consolidated European & North American Railroad had inflated its bonds. That was down in Maine in 1881. I gave a very learned opinion there on that subject. Mr. Otis was asked for his opinion, and he said he hadn't time to deliver the opinion, "but here is an opinion, written by a young friend in whom I have great confidence," etc.

That led to my being retained in that Consolidated European & North American litigation,[20] which took about ten years, nearly, and which

17. *Philip Allen & Sons v. Woonsocket Company*, 13 R.I. 146 (R.I. 1880).

18. *Dormitzer v. Illinois & St. Louis Bridge Co.*, 6 F. 217 (D. Massachusetts, 1881).

19. 130 Mass. 325

20. *Norton v. European & N. A. R. Co.*, 32 F. 865 (D. Maine 1887).

gave us a good deal of money for those days, and which made me familiar with railroad questions, and took me down into Maine. I got to know the federal court down in Maine, and the lawyers there. And I also went down into New Brunswick.

And meanwhile I was getting pretty well known around here. In 1881 Ezra Thayer's father, James B. Thayer,[21] who was one of my teachers, was expecting to take his sabbatical year, and he asked me to give the course on Evidence. I was disposed to do it. Then he changed his mind—postponed going. He said he would want me to do it the next year. That gave me a chance to work it up for another year. So, I did work it up, and when he went abroad, I went out and gave the course on Evidence. That was in 1882–3. It made a very pronounced success—quite a striking impression at Harvard.

In that winter Mr. Holmes was the professor. He resigned in midwinter—Christmas week—to take a place on the Supreme Court. He was to be appointed before Ben Butler[22] came in. They wanted me to come out as assistant professor, with the promise of a professorship.

I had been intimate with Professor Langdell, who was a great friend of mine, but I said, "If this were ten years later, I would be inclined to come, but I don't feel that I want to come now."

He said, "In ten years you may not get the chance." But I said I would rather take the chance of not getting it when I wanted it than to take it when I didn't want it. So, I didn't do it.

During all this time I had taken a very great interest in the law school. As a matter of fact, I had been instrumental in getting the money for the very professorship which put Mr. Holmes there.

One of the young men to whom I had taught law was William [F. Weld], who was the grandson of William G. [Weld], a very rich ship owner. The grandfather died and left Billy [Weld] three million dollars. Billy was afterwards a member of the Polo Club and had a beautiful place near the Country Club.

21. James Bradley Thayer (1831–1902) was a long-time professor at Harvard Law School. His son Ezra Ripley Thayer (1866–1915) graduated from Harvard Law School in 1891, and after a short stint in Brandeis's law firm became the Dean of Harvard Law School.

22. Benjamin F. Butler (1818–1893) was a lawyer, Civil War general, military governor of New Orleans and congressman. He was governor of Massachusetts from January 1883 to January 1884.

I knew of the desire to get Holmes out there, and I happened to meet [Weld][23] just after he had inherited this money. I got hold of him and told him we wanted to establish a professorship. He wanted to know how much. I said, "Ninety thousand dollars." I had been talking with Professor Thayer about it. He said, "Well, I would like to meet Professor Thayer." I said, "Tomorrow morning." On the following morning, Saturday, he saw Professor Thayer and agreed to put up the ninety thousand to establish the professorship.

Then I helped raise some more money for the library from Nickerson, one of the fellows I had taught, and from one or two other sources. I had been giving a good deal of thought to the Law School. And in 1885, when it came to the time of the preparation for the 250th anniversary, Professor Thayer took up with me the matter of doing something for the school. It was then in rather a parlous position. The new Langdellian system of teaching law by cases had made its way very slowly. The old-fashioned lawyers protested very much against it, and the result had been that the school, instead of growing, had gone back.

During my two years there were about 190 in the school. When they had a three-year course, nearly ten years later, they had about 150 or 160. The school was in need of money and in need of students. I talked with Professor Thayer to the effect that they had a remarkably good thing but that people didn't know about it—that the thing to do was to make it known, and we concluded to get up the Law School Association. I entered upon that task with very great diligence, and called in Winthrop Wade, who was one of the students while I was out there with the class of '84. I taught Evidence in the second-year class of '82–3. He was of that class and had been a good student. I knew him well, and met him one day at lunch, and told him about it. He said he would come in as treasurer, and he was a faithful worker. I planned to reach out to every state and get hold of all the people. We had the 250th anniversary, a great meeting, at which, as I remember it, Justice Holmes delivered the address.[24]

---

23. The manuscript says William G. Wells but this is likely a transcription error. It was William F. Weld (1855–1893) who donated the money. The Weld Professor of Law Chair continues to be a position to this day.

24. The address was published as "The Use of Law Schools" in Oliver Wendell Holmes, Jr., *Speeches* (Boston: Little, Brown and Company, 1881), pp. 28–40.

We built up the organization, and the effect was marvelous. The school began to grow very rapidly. Soon it was embarrassed by growth. It ran up to 300, 400, 500, 600 students. I kept working as long as it was desirable to have it grow, and then stopped working.

Meanwhile, the *Law Review* had been started. Mr. Nutter[25] was, I think, the first editor-in-chief. They couldn't make the thing go. I suggested the thing to do was to get publicity. People must know what the *Law Review* was. I got some money from Mr. Warren and Mr. Hecht and concluded to distribute among all the member of the Association who were not already subscribers copies of the *Review* for one year. I said, "One issue won't do any good. Let these fellows have every number for a year, and then you have some chance."

So, I got the money for that, and the plan proved a great success. That put the *Review* on its feet.

I then became trustee of the *Law Review* and have remained so ever since. Mr. Nutter, James Barr Ames,[26] and I were the trustees during Mr. Ames' life.

It was largely my service to the Law School, I suppose, which induced them afterwards to give me the honorary degree of A.M. [Master of Arts] in 1891.

That was really the important public work that I did at that time. I spent a tremendous amount of time and got in touch with lawyers all over the country. I don't know whether we still have the correspondence, or whether I sent it to Cambridge when I ceased to be secretary. But our letter books would show the tremendous correspondence which I conducted.

But I had taken some part in public work from the very start. The first thing I did when I came here, which was as early as October 1879, I first became a visitor for the Associated Charities. After a few weeks, I became a member of the Executive Committee for Ward 8, of which George Wigglesworth and Dr. Charles P. Putnam were also members. Dr. Putnam was chairman, and I think George Wigglesworth was after-

25. George Read Nutter (1863–1937) graduated from Harvard Law School in 1889 and joined Brandeis's law firm in the following year. Nutter was actually the editor-in-chief of the journal during its second year.

26. James Barr Ames (1846–1910) graduated from Harvard Law School in 1872 and then spent the rest of his life teaching there.

wards chairman. I went on that as the most advanced thing in helping poor people that there was.

Then I went into the Civil Service Reform movement—composed of the people who afterward were the Mugwumps—the most advanced thing in the political world.

I also went into the social municipal work with Curtis Guild in Ward 9, where I then lived.

Then there was formed the Citizens Association, that Herbert Harding was in. That didn't do very great things, and I went into the Municipal League, with Samuel B. Capen.

All those local reform organizations were composed of Boston's elite, but they never accomplished very much. In my connection with the Citizens Association, I had my first relations with the street railway problem.[27] I then came to many of the very conclusions that I was afterwards able to work out—that the street railways were getting a great deal out of the public for nothing.

On one of these occasions—I think '92 or '93—when I appeared at a meeting and spoke against allowing the Tremont Street tracks to be extended into the Common, which was then proposed as a means of meeting the congestion, I stated that on the contrary the railroad was getting so much out of the city, that out of its earnings it ought to provide some other way to meet the congestion.

It was largely the speech on that occasion, I think, at which Mrs. Alice N. Lincoln was present, that induced her to get me to represent her in the public institutions matter.[28] I had been acting a good deal in public institution matters and generally in public charitable matters, because I became intimate with Mr. and Mrs. Glendower Evans[29] shortly after they were married, in 1882 or 1883—was intimate with Glen from then until 1886 when he died. Immediately after his death Dr. Putnam, who was his physician, got Mrs. Evans appointed to the board of State

---

27. Brandeis fought a long battle resisting the Boston Elevated Railway Company's attempts to monopolize Boston's public transportation.

28. Alice N. Lincoln (1853–1926) was a Boston philanthropist. At her urging, Brandeis held a number of public meetings in an effort to improve conditions at the Boston Almshouse and Hospital.

29. Glen Glendower Evans (1856–1886) was a lawyer at Shattuck, Holmes and Munroe. After his death, his wife Elizabeth Glendower Evans (1856–1937), became one of the Brandeises' closest friends.

Institutions, really to mitigate her terrible sorrow. That put her mind on impersonal things, and she began at once to consult me about all of her charitable propositions.

So, I knew all of these things beginning with '88. Afterwards, in '90 Mayor Matthews had occasion to appoint a committee to investigate our institutions, on account of the holler that had been made by Mrs. Lincoln. Mrs. Evans was appointed a member of that committee, so that I was associated with all of those problems. That led up to the public institutions hearing. Of course, when I got into the matter, I hadn't any idea that I was in for a long period. At that time, I had already a very large practice. Reed and Curtis were counsel for the officials there (Curtis afterwards became Mayor) and they thought I couldn't give the matter attention, and so the hearings began to be dragged out. There were 84 hearings. At most of them I was present. Then the question came up as to what I should do. I made up my mind I would charge Mrs. Lincoln a reasonable fee. I charged her $3000. The city was charged $15,000 for much less service than I rendered.

I made up my mind then to give away my share of that money and not to keep any of it for myself. I made one gift to the Children's Aid, one to the Associated Charities, one to the Municipal League (with which I was then connected), one to the Ethical Society in New York, and some other gifts.

Long before that I had become well known here, and had been invited, back in 1888 or 1889, to deliver the course on Business Law at the Institute of Technology by President Walker, but really through Alexander Wheeler, of Hutchins and Wheeler, who was an important man there. I intended to deliver it in 1891–2, but I had to postpone it until 1892–3, and I delivered it three years, with one intermission.[30]

But before that, in 1889, Mr. Edwin H. Abbot had a very important case in Washington coming up in the fall of that year. The counsel whom he had relied upon to take the case couldn't take it. It had also rankled with him that he had been one of the stockholders in that Illinois Bridge Co. case. He had made up his mind that when he wanted counsel he would come to me, so he asked me to prepare the brief in the Wisconsin

30. Brandeis's business lectures have been published. See Robert F. Cochran, Jr., editor, *Louis D. Brandeis's MIT Lectures on Law (1892–1894)* (Durham: Carolina Academic Press, 2012).

Central case.[31] But he was at first a little fearful that I couldn't handle it, and he retained Judge Jeremiah Smith who had been on the New Hampshire Supreme Court, and was then at Harvard as a professor, and an excellent lawyer, to be senior counsel. So, I prepared the brief and then they concluded that I was the man to argue it. In fact, I was the only man who did argue, because Senator Spooner, who was to be on the other side, didn't arrive in time to argue the case. I submitted the brief, and the case was won. That led to my getting other cases for the Wisconsin Central, and becoming their Eastern counsel, and afterwards counsel for the receivers.

But in the meantime, our business had developed very much throughout the country, and the business in Boston began to grow—my personal business as distinguished from Mr. Warren's. Mr. Warren had practically retired from the firm—not actually—but practically in 1888. The firm was not dissolved until 1897. Mr. Warren had taken no active part since 1888. Of course, I became pretty widely known during that period. I had written somewhat:

"Trust Estates."[32]

And at the time of our anniversary, I had written the article on "The Harvard Law School" in *The Green Bag*.[33] Then came "The Right to Privacy,"[34] which attracted a good deal of attention.

Mr. Warren and I had worked out largely together the Watuppa Pond decision.[35]

By the early '90's I had a good deal of business and had appeared so often in different parts of the country that I was pretty well known to the Bar outside of Massachusetts. You [Grady][36] came in 1894. Soon after

---

31. *Wisconsin Central R. Co. v. Price County*, 133 U.S. 496 (1896). This case was Brandeis's first appearance before the U.S. Supreme Court.

32. Louis D. Brandeis, "Liability of Trust Estates on Contracts Made for Their Benefit," *American Law Review* 15 (1881): 449–462.

33. Louis D. Brandeis, "The Harvard Law School," *Green Bag* 1 (1889): 10–25, and also on pages 145–166 in this volume.

34. Samuel D. Warren and Louis D. Brandeis, "The Right to Privacy," *Harvard Law Review* 4 (1890): 193–220.

35. Samuel D. Warren and Louis D. Brandeis, "The Watuppa Pond Cases," *Harvard Law Review* 2 (1888): 195–211.

36. Alice Harriet Grady (1873–1934) was hired by Brandeis to be his secretary shortly after she graduated from business school. After he joined the Supreme Court, she became deputy commissioner of Savings Bank Insurance.

that I had so much business I began to withdraw from the trial of ordinary cases and to go into the special things.

The thing I used to see Judge Bradley about mostly—he was a great buyer of pictures, and he would hesitate about buying anything. He liked to have me go with him to see the picture before he bought it.

One of the reasons I was taken up as I was in Boston society was because of the culture which I had. I knew more about art and music than most of the people did. Boston did give this to me: I was then a very serious minded individual, with terribly [the manuscript has a blank space here] views of life, and Puritan ideals. Boston came nearer my ideal than anything I had ever found anywhere else.

The real fact is that I haven't changed as much as these people have whom I used to be with. The old Puritan New England has vanished. Early New England was built up on the Old Testament, and I think it was that a good deal which made me feel so much at home in New England. The reason why I was at home everywhere in the circles in which I moved was that very thing. As Albert Otis said, "You are of older family than these people."

There was John Gray. The Thayers. And the Thayers were great friends of Emerson. Also, partly through Mr. Warren, I was thrown in with all of Boston society. Instead of having the trouble a fellow usually has to gain admittance, I was simply taken up. Was a great deal at the home of Mrs. James T. Fields, which was a sort of literary center.

Then I was with musical people all the time. I was one of the first to rejoice in the Symphony Concerts.

Quite intimate with Hughes.

In 1889 and 1890, the high brows undertook to take the *Boston Post* and make it a worthy Bostonian sheet. I, with Joe Lee as representing the Lee-Higginsons, and Mr. Hughes, as representing the Forbses, went in to try to run that. We lost what money there was, through Mr. E. M. Bacon,[37] who died recently. He was the editor at that time and lost our money for us, until Mr. Grozier came in and bought it out. Then in 1907, Mr. Grozier asked me whether I would become editor of his paper.

37. Edwin Monroe Bacon (1844–1916) had been the editor of a number of newspapers before taking over the *Post*. He died on February 24, 1916, so this interview must have taken place after that date.

I met the Child family through a very intimate friend of ours, Edith Harlan, daughter of Justice Harlan, who married a brother of H. Walter Child.[38] I became acquainted with the Child family in 1877. I went up there to Worcester.

The feeling that these people have is that I was right in the midst of them and was treated as well as anybody could possibly be treated, and that I withdrew from them—that I didn't believe in their ways.

Mrs. Frank Peabody's brother, Mr. Edward B. Bailey, was a client of mine—a large shipping house. Used often to dine with the Frank Peabodys and go to the Symphony concerts with them. That was back in the 1880's. Then afterwards, I attacked their pet enterprises, and gradually it began to spread to other people. Savings Bank Insurance[39] alienated a good many people. And in the interval, I had alienated a good many in the gas matter.[40] For instance, Laurence Minot had been a great friend while we were fighting the Elevated Railway. But when we got on to gas and electricity, he became violent, and when we got onto the New Haven[41] he became rampant.

The first person who called on Mrs. Brandeis when we came to Boston was Mrs. Henry L. Higginson. And the first weekend party we were invited to was to Mrs. Frank Lowell's.

The thing that got my mind specifically on to labor problems—the first I knew very much about it—had been gradually picking up some knowledge in connection with the Haverhill shoe strike—the Homestead strike[42] in connection with the lectures for the Institute in 1882.

---

38. Brandeis knew the Harlans from his childhood days in Louisville. Not only was he friends with Edith Harlan (1857–1882) but he also worked closely with her brother, James S. Harlan (1861–1927), when he was a commissioner on the Interstate Commerce Commission. Brandeis was also instrumental in helping the Brandeis School of Law acquire John Marshall Harlan's papers.

39. In order to protect poor families that were being victimized by insurance companies, Brandeis helped establish the Savings Bank Life Insurance Company of Massachusetts, which is still in business today.

40. Various businessmen consolidated the companies that provided gas to Boston. Brandeis alienated many of his former allies when he chose not to oppose the consolidation but instead ensured that the new company charged fair rates.

41. Brandeis fought a years long battle to keep the New Haven Railroad from monopolizing all New England transportation. Many of Brandeis's former friends were in favor of the monopoly.

42. The violence at the shoe factories around Haverhill, Massachusetts in 1894–95 and at the Homestead Steel mill in 1892 shocked Brandeis and influenced his thinking about unions.

I always felt I had a truer sense of the value of money than any of the people that I went around with. It was always easy for me to earn money, and I never let money earn me. I wasn't reckless with money, like some of the other people. I saw the value of it because it gave a man freedom. On the other hand, I was never willing to sacrifice my freedom for money. The only use that it could have would be:

To give freedom

To do what you wanted to do

To be what you wanted to be

To accomplish what you wanted to accomplish

You know that I have been extremely free in paying out money for any purpose that I believed in. I was just as economical on the other hand and didn't waste a cent on something I didn't believe in.

It was Emerson who said—what his friends are apt to forget—it struck me as a boy—"Spend for your expense and retrench in the expense which is not yours." The moment that I arrived in the practice of law at the point of having more than I needed, I began to find somebody to do the things that I didn't believe were educating. When I got Mr. Hoar[43] in here the first time, it was to do certain work in our office that I thought he could do that would save my time. I would rather study. I didn't have much more than I was spending. I had enough to have a pleasant margin and decided that I would never do any work unnecessarily that was not educating, and that whatever I did would be to make me able to do something else better. I never worked less hard. As you know, I was working harder, almost all the time. But whenever I found that the work was taking something out of me instead of my taking something out of the work in the way of growth, I stopped doing it.

Of course, I had to be extremely careful of my health because I was always going the limit. I had had several lessons which I thought taught me what the limit was. I had the lesson with my eyes. After I began to stop using my eyes, and used my head to save my eyes, I found there was such a thing as misusing your head. Then I got nervous indigestion, which took hold of me for about seven years. So that I had to be careful for about seven years—until about 1886. Then I thought I reached a time where I was in fine shape to do what I wanted, and I landed in 1901 with insomnia, which occupied me for . . .

43. D. Blakeley Hoar (1855–1923) was the first lawyer to join Warren and Brandeis.

I used to run right along during one of those attacks, so that by Saturday noon I was all worn out, and it was a question whether the reservoir could be filled by Monday morning.

I, who had been a singularly sociable individual, began to find that if I wanted to do my work I must withdraw. I used to go practically into retreat. My habit of avoiding people was not that I was not sociably inclined, but it was a question of doing one thing or another. So, I began to lead a pretty solitary life. I made up my mind to work, and said, "If I work, I am going to make that work pleasurable." And whenever I found that work was not a pleasure, then I knew I was in bad shape, time to run away. You have seen me run away once in a while.

Dunbar in 1887. Nutter in 1889. Thayer in 1892. I was in close touch with the law school and selected the men who had high standing in the school.[44]

It was important for me that I should have clients. My clients didn't have a lawyer. I made up my mind: "I will give my advice for results, not for money."

44. The document gets a little vague here. Presumably Brandeis and Grady were discussing the growth of Warren and Brandeis. William Harrison Dunbar (1862–1935) actually joined the firm in 1888 while Nutter joined it in 1890.

21

# Conversation with Uncle Louis

*After ascending to the Supreme Court in 1916, Brandeis rarely gave interviews. As a result, it is difficult to discern how Brandeis felt on many issues of the day. His letters give some insight into his opinions and his personality, but by the 1920s his letters became shorter and more business-like and therefore give almost no hint of Brandeis's personality. The charm of this transcription is that it provides a rare glimpse of what Brandeis was like when he was relaxed. Throughout his life, Brandeis was sought out by the luminaries of the day for his company. This transcription gives a brief impression of what one of those conversations was like.*

*This transcription of a conversation on September 15, 1939, was presumably made by Brandeis's niece Fanny (identified as "F".) The other two participants are Brandeis's wife Alice ("Aunt Alice") and British economist Redvers Opie, who was attached to the British Embassy at the time. The setting is probably Brandeis's apartment in Washington. The punctuation and notation of the original has been retained which may make for confusing reading, but with a little work it should not be too difficult to determine which quotes are Brandeis's.*

*The transcription is held in folder A1-7 in the University of Louisville Brandeis Collection.*

"Louis[1] would change the Neutrality law if he were in Congress, how would you vote?"

"I don't know, but perhaps the next few weeks will show how to vote."

"It's the same war, isn't it?"

"Well, it's certainly the same people making war; from what we know of 25 years ago we know what to expect."

(Redvers) "I have no patience with those who blame this one the Treaty of Versailles."

"Oh—the Treaty of Versailles has little to do with this war. There were injustices, but it is the same thing in the German people which provoked the other war that has brought this one—in that sense it is the same war. And assuming that the Allies win, what hope is there for the next peace?"

(F.) "That's what I say—the war depresses me, but the peace treaty depresses me even more."

"What can be done with such a people? Even if the treaty were the best that the wisdom of man and virtue of man can devise, what can be done with the German people? If it were the Germans to treat with them, they would kill everyone." (Then a long sentence—not verbatim.) "No other such situation in the history of the civilized world. Nations have waged war on a grievance, sometimes manufactured, but to evict a whole group of people, robbing them at the same time shows a reversion to the Iroquois. If the Germans had followed the benign custom of Governments in invoking the right of eminent domain and arrived at a just system of recompense, the incensed feelings against them would have been largely reduced."

Redvers thinks the special session is to decide if America will go to war. Aunt Alice emphatically says no. Uncle Louis says it is impossible to tell what this country will do, as it is impossible to tell what will happen in Europe.

Redvers says when Hitler has cleaned up Eastern Europe and pretty well flattened out France and England, America will go into the war. As a Britisher, he wishes we would now; as an American he thinks we will on purely sentimental reasons, without rationalizing, and he thinks the neutrality legislation is beside the point.

Uncle Louis said one man close to the President told him he is apt to get his neutrality revisions through. LDB said "You mean you think he

1. Presumably they are referring to Brandeis's nephew Louis Brandeis Wehle.

will?" "No. I said he is apt to." However, another, very close says he will get it. The Republicans will be with him. LDB doubts if it can be a short session.

"All I can do is let people talk to me and imagine I help them. I don't—but..."

"No—the fifties are the best years—Justice Holmes didn't agree, he thought the seventies, but then, for all his philosophy, Justice Holmes worried."

"Did you ever worry?"

"No, never—not even when I had the trouble with my eyes. That was when I was about nineteen. The doctor told me I had better give up all idea of the law. I told Father and he said to try another doctor (I had been to one in Boston and in Cincinnati) so I went to Dr. Knapp in New York. And he said to go on—if I were a nervous woman, it would be different, but with my temperament I could go on. It was a strain from too much use with the wrong kind of light, probably, flickering, uncertain light—there was never anything organically wrong with my eyes."

"I sometimes think I might have had more education—eighteen and nineteen when I was in Law School. But I am a great believer in starting young. The enthusiasm and fire of youth means more than maturity. So, I think the fifties are the best. By that time, I had been working thirty years and the experience of those years was there. I never worried."

"If you didn't worry about yourself, didn't you worry about the world or about people you cared about?"

"I always went on the principle of 'Do what you can and hope for the best.' I worked on the problem at hand. All those years before I went on the Court, that was my philosophy."

"Did you ever expect you'd go on the Court?"

"I never thought about it. I never worked for anything. I merely went ahead with what I had to do."

"'Ten years is very little time in which to accomplish anything. President Eliott always said twenty years—twenty years would show what had grown and developed."

# Index